Contents

Adolf
Schlatter

Adolf Schlatter

*A Biography of Germany's
Premier Biblical Theologian*

Werner Neuer

Translated by
Robert W. Yarbrough

BakerBooks

A Division of Baker Book House Co
Grand Rapids, Michigan 49516

©1995 by Robert W. Yarbrough

First German paperback edition published and copyrighted 1988 by R.
Brockhaus Verlag Wuppertal.

First English paperback edition published by Baker Books
a division of Baker Book House Company
P.O. Box 6287, Grand Rapids, MI 49516-6287
Printed in the United States of America

Library of Congress Cataloging-in-Publication Data

Neuer, Werner, 1951–
   [Adolf Schlatter. English]
   Adolf Schlatter : a biography of Germany's premier biblical theologian /
Werner Neuer ; translated by Robert W. Yarbrough.
      p.   cm.
   Includes bibliographical references and index.
   ISBN 0-8010-2069-7 (paper)
   1. Schlatter, Adolf von, 1852–1938. 2. New Testament scholars—
Germany—Biography. 3. Theologians—Germany—Biography. I. Title.
BS2351.S3N4813   1996
230'.092—dc20   95-43427
[B]

Photographs 1, 5, 6, 7, 12, 15, 19, 22, 26, 27, 31, 34, 35, 36, 37, 39, 40, 41, 42,
43, 46, 49, 50, 51, 52, 54, 55, 56, 57, 58, 59, and 60 used by permission of
Theodor Schlatter; photographs 3, 4, 13, 25, 28, 29, and 45 used by permission
of Landeskirchliches Archiv, Stuttgart, Germany; photograph 48 used
by permission of Frau Lilo Brunner; photographs 16, 17, 20, and 21 used by
permission of Bergerbibliothek Bern, Bern, Switzerland; photograph 47
used by permission of Werner Neumeister; photograph 24 used by permission
of Stiftung Pommern, Kiel, Germany; photograph 32 used by permission of
Ullstein Bilderdienst, Berlin, Germany; photograph 8 used by permission
of Universitätsbibliothek Portraitsammlung, Basle, Switzerland; photograph
33 used by permission of Universitätsarchiv Tübingen; photograph 53 used by
permission of Universitätsbibliothek Tübingen.

Appendix B from Adolf Schlatter, *Das christliche Dogma*, 4th ed. (1984), pp.
303–12 (including notes on pp. 575–76). © Calwer Verlag Stuttgart. Used by
permission of Calwer Verlag Stuttgart. Appendix C from Robert Morgan,
Nature of New Testament Theology, Studies in Biblical Theology, 2nd series,
no. 25, SCM Press, 1973, pp. 117–66. Used by permission of SCM Press Ltd.,
London. Appendix D originally appeared in the *Asbury Theological Journal* as
"Atheistic Methods in Theology." Used by permission of the *Asbury
Theological Journal*.

Foreword

I am delighted to see this biography of Adolf Schlatter appear in English. Although it provides only the merest taste of the multifaceted character of Schlatter's career, and although it can only hint at the significance of his work, it is nonetheless entirely welcome. The addition of samples from Schlatter's own pen measurably enhances what Werner Neuer has written about him.

The anomalies of Schlatter's career, which spanned a full half century as active lecturer, preacher, and writer, have been responsible for the relative neglect of his work since he died immediately before the start of the Second World War. Schlatter was far too conservative in his approach to the New Testament, and to Christian theology in general, to win a reputation in the university world in which he labored so earnestly. Yet he was also far too scholarly in his approach to problems of theological method and far too willing to engage the leading thinkers of his day to make much of an impact on the popular pietism of the German-speaking world with which he shared so much. The result was a contribution that has never received its due—despite the incredibly wide range of Schlatter's publications, the profundity of his Christian reflection on theological method, and the acuity of the criticism he directed against the prevailing theological assumptions of his day (assumptions that, despite much that has subsequently intervened, still influence the university study of theology in contemporary North America and Britain as well as in continental Europe).

I cannot pretend to know Schlatter or his work well, but I have been greatly encouraged by what I have learned about

Foreword

him, largely through the efforts of Robert Yarbrough, who has provided this English translation of Neuer's introductory biography. The insights displayed in the essays by Schlatter that are contained in this book suggest why his work may be nearly as relevant now as during his own lifetime. For example, Schlatter's criticism of the notion that the university study of religion requires the presupposition of atheism is extraordinarily shrewd. It provides, in fact, a discussion of such questions worthy to be considered with Peter Berger's influential essay on "methodological atheism" that appeared as an appendix to *The Sacred Canopy* in 1967.

Schlatter's thoughts on the meaning of "science" in that same essay are equally noteworthy. Above all, his ringing assertion—"Science is first seeing *(Sehen)* and secondly seeing and thirdly seeing and again and again seeing"—is as timely an appeal as when it was first made, especially since Schlatter by no means held to a simplistic or positivistic view of academic investigation.

Finally, it is altogether fitting that this book includes also one of Schlatter's short reflections on prayer. It is a mark of the singular usefulness of Schlatter and his ideas for the contemporary moment that he offers such a positive example of how to combine the academic rigor necessary to function in the modern academy with the living piety required to keep faith with Christ and his church. Schlatter's unusual integrity as a "thinking pietist" or a "pious thinker" is one of the virtues that most recommends him to those, like myself, who are late in recognizing his importance.

This biography and its bits from Schlatter can only be a beginning. But those who read carefully the pages that follow may be forgiven a prayer that more of Schlatter's writings will soon be made available in English and, even more, that Schlatter's singular combination of faith and learning may find many imitators at a time when that combination is just as desperately needed as it was in Schlatter's own day.

Mark Noll

Translator's Preface

This volume is valuable on two counts. First, it contains the only biography yet to be published on one of Christianity's truly seminal (and neglected) post-Enlightenment thinkers: Adolf Schlatter (1852–1938). At a time when awareness of both Protestant liberalism's theological inadequacy and evangelicalism's intellectual poverty have become acute,[1] the publication of even a starter-biography that helps access Schlatter's formidable theological and intellectual acuity is a welcome event. A canny biblical conservative who taught alongside arch-liberal Adolf von Harnack in Berlin—and won Harnack's respect as both academic peer and personal friend—may have something to teach participants in the academic and ecclesiastical culture wars of today.

Additionally, the appendixes of this volume contain valuable primary source readings. Schlatter has remained largely unknown in English-speaking circles because of a dearth of translations of his writings. Following a time-line synopsis of Schlatter's life (Appendix A), the reader will find (in Appendix B) Robert Morgan's translation of Schlatter's reflections on how New Testament exegesis and theology ought to go about its work. Schlatter tackles broad methodological issues

---

1. On liberalism's inadequacies, see, e.g., Thomas Oden, Requiem: A Lament in Three Movements (Nashville: Abingdon, 1995); Alister McGrath, Evangelicalism and the Future of Christianity (Downers Grove: InterVarsity, 1995). On evangelicalism's poverty, see Mark Noll, The Scandal of the Evangelical Mind (Grand Rapids/Leicester: Eerdmans/InterVarsity, 1994).

that are by no means passé today.[2] These include the need for careful linguistic and historical study as prelude and guide to theological reflection, the inevitability of theological overtones and agendas in biblical interpretation, how interpretation can arrive at conclusions that amount to more than mere recounting of an observer's subjective impressions, and the respective distinctive contributions of "Christian" and "secular" viewpoints in the overall human quest for understanding, especially of the Bible.

Next, in Appendix C, come vintage reflections on prayer from Schlatter's one-volume dogmatics.[3] This is by no means the sum of his thoughts on the subject. But it does offer a window into his careful and pithy mode of expression. We find here exposition that is both intellectually rigorous and spiritually uplifting (or convicting, as the case may be). Perhaps this sample will whet readers' appetites for more extensive exposure to Schlatter's insights on other topics. Schlatter would no doubt have hoped that his words would also spur readers on to prayer that is more productive in its basis, intent, and outcome, because it is more confident in Christ, carefully reflected, and theologically informed.

Finally, Appendix D renders Schlatter's response to Paul Jäger's insistence that the language of Zion must abide by the conventions of the denizens of Athens. Not to work within the doctrines established—or sometimes simply asserted—by secular "science," Jäger insists, is to give up the right to participate in serious discussion in the modern academy. Schlatter counters that such "science," with all due praise for its avowed empirical aims, is just an atheist substitute for the dogmatic ecclesial authority that the Enlightenment jettisoned. Science is first seeing, then seeing, then seeing some more, Schlatter urges, and to interpret biblical (or any other)

---

2. Note the very different answers given to precisely these questions in Heikki Räisänen, Beyond New Testament Theology (London/Philadelphia: SCM/Trinity Press International, 1990).

3. The translation that appeared as "Das christliche Dogma—Prayer," London Quarterly and Holburn Review 170 (1945):420–25, is defective.

data in the light of "scientific" doctrines not derived from careful scrutiny of those data is not only bad exegesis; it is poor science. Significantly, Schlatter's case is not dependent on a commitment to biblical literalism; it rests rather on a carefully reflected critical realist epistemology that he sets forth in numerous essays and several books on philosophy and metaphysics, as Neuer's biography makes clear. It also rests on a tacit openness to the presence of the transcendent yet personal God in the sphere of time and matter that is reminiscent of Augustine, the Reformers, and Jonathan Edwards, though this is a connection that Neuer does not bring out.

Here is an approach to knowledge, theology, and their integration that rivals the fruitfulness of Scottish common-sense realism for dogmatics without falling prey to Scottish realism's liabilities. Schlatter has a very different response to Kantianism than the scientistic one of the Old Princeton School, for example, and he owes much more to J. G. Hamann (by way of Franz von Baader) than to Francis Bacon or Thomas Reid (as important as Bacon and Reid continue to be in their place—which is probably not furnishing the central platform for Christian dogmatics). Schlatter's suggestive response to Jäger (whose views continue today among theologians like David Tracy, Schubert Ogden, and Delwin Brown) may prove stimulating for those currently committed to the task of revivifying Christian scholarship in academic settings exclusionary of all viewpoints except those sanctioned by the reigning critical elite.

The appendixes practically exhaust the stock of Schlatter's writings currently available in English.[4] For this reason alone this book should be a valuable tool for students of Schlatter for many years to come.

Calls to learn from the scholarship—and heart—of Adolf Schlatter have sounded for some years now. Voices as diverse

4. The growing list of exceptions includes Schlatter's review of Karl Barth's Romans commentary in J. M. Robinson, ed., The Beginnings of Dialectical Theology (Richmond: John Knox, 1968), 121–25. See also Schlatter's The Church in the New Testament Period, trans. Paul P. Levertoff (London: SPCK, 1955). Apparently the only work

Translator's Preface

as Ward Gasque, James Dunn, Robert Morgan, Stephen Neill, Martin Hengel, Peter Stuhlmacher, Helmut Thielicke, and numerous others have commended Schlatter as a first-rate thinker. Werner Neuer has performed a valuable service in producing this brief but highly illuminating vignette of a scholar-churchman whose greatest contribution to the church in its ongoing struggle with (post) modernity could still lie in the future.

---

by Schlatter translated into English during his lifetime was "The Attitude of German Protestant Theology to the Bible," Constructive Quarterly 2 (1914):99–100. More recently, Schlatter's critical Romans commentary is reportedly available from Hendrickson Publishers in a translation by Siegfried Schatzmann. The section on Scripture from Schlatter's dogmatics appears in an appendix of Stephen E. Dintaman, Creative Grace: Faith and History in the Theology of Adolf Schlatter (New York et al.: Peter Lang, 1993), but is not always to be trusted in its renderings of Schlatter's difficult German.

Looking to the future, Baker Book House has commissioned the translation of Schlatter's two-volume New Testament theology, which is being undertaken by Andreas Köstenberger.

Preface to Original Edition

Adolf Schlatter (1852–1938) is rightly regarded as one of the great biblical theologians of the twentieth century. His wide-ranging theological writings sought to pass along the message of Holy Scripture as faithfully and comprehensively as possible. Schlatter wished to take Scripture into account especially at those points where it tended to be overlooked— whether by fashionable modern thought or by church tradition. He was best known for his New Testament interpretation, and his reputation spread far beyond Germany.

His biblical exposition has come to be regarded as practically "classic" in rank; it bears comparison with that of such other greats as Augustine, Luther, Calvin, and Bengel. His nine scholarly New Testament commentaries continue to furnish New Testament specialists with a wealth of stimulating insights right down to the present day. At the lay level his ten-volume commentary on the whole New Testament is still familiar to many Bible-reading Christians. But Schlatter left a permanent mark in other fields besides New Testament exegesis and the study of ancient Judaism, in both of which he was an expert. Many of his over four hundred publications were devoted to a range of disciplines, including church history, dogmatics, ethics, practical theology, and philosophy.

His influence on theology and church life in twentieth-century German-speaking Protestantism should by no means be minimized, even if his contribution has not received as much attention since World War II as it did during his lifetime. In any case, no other German-speaking theologian of his generation comes even close to having so many books still in print: more than thirty of his writings remain available. In view of the indisputable significance of Schlatter's life and work for evangelical theology, it is no wonder that the call for a scholarly account of his life has sounded loudly since his death on May 19, 1938. This little book does not seek to do justice to that call. Its aim is quite different, even if it is the first Schlatter biography ever written, and even if it is informed by long years of painstaking research (including three years' study of Schlatter's unpublished letters and other papers).

The aim is rather to make the basic features of his life and spiritual-theological intentions accessible to a larger circle of readers. I have accordingly dispensed with footnotes; most quotations come from Schlatter's own remarks, published or unpublished. It is hoped that this will result in the highest possible degree of authenticity and vividness in what follows.

Because this study is a sketch rather than a complete portrait, the reader will have to put up with considerable gaps in Schlatter's life. I was quite conscious that such difficulties would be part of this undertaking. I have chosen to focus on those matters that throw light on Schlatter as a *person* and as a *Christian*. Schlatter the *theologian* and his theological writings proper recede into the background by comparison. One result of this, for instance, is that Schlatter's effect as a theology professor in Germany receives less attention than the broad sweep of his earlier years in Switzerland. The fuller story of his scholarly achievement must await publication of the more technical biography scheduled for publication in Germany shortly.

In spite of the limits of this book, I trust that I have produced a story that conveys to both theologians and non-theologians a graphic impression of Schlatter's life and work. Even those quite familiar with Schlatter may read it with profit. (For the scholarly community, in my comprehensive scientific biography due out any day I hope to do justice to

Preface to Original Edition

Schlatter's significance for theology and church history and to fulfill the demand for a full account of his life that has sounded now for decades.)

My thanks first of all to my wife, who has aided my work on this book with her understanding and interest. Thanks too to my children, who had to do without their father during a considerable portion of my annual vacation. I also thank Rev. Christoph Cassetti, who generously opened the workroom of his manse in Liechtenstein to me during summer holidays. I am very much indebted to the late Rev. Hans Stroh for his long-standing support and stimulation in my Schlatter studies. I likewise thank Mr. Theodor Schlatter of Besigheim for kindly making available the biggest share of this book's many photos. The Schlatter Foundation generously supported my research of Schlatter's papers over many years. Finally, I must mention Mr. Bernhard Müller and the Verein zur Erziehung und Förderung e. V. (Stuttgart), without whose financial support my studies would not have been possible. I also wish to thank the long-standing guardian of Schlatter's papers, Rev. Ernst Bock of Korntal, for his help in assembling photographs.

I dedicate this book to the Protestant and evangelical congregations of Walddorf and Häslach in gratitude for their good-intentioned and affectionate participation in my work as associate pastor. Here I must expressly mention Pastor Martin Eberle, my supervisor during my first months in the pastorate, who with fraternal understanding bore with this book's composition as it inevitably took time away from my pastoral duties.

WERNER NEUER
Gomaringen, Germany

1

Childhood and Youth in St. Gallen, Switzerland

Adolf Schlatter hailed from a venerable Swiss family whose presence in St. Gallen can be traced back to the fifteenth century. Already in 1461 we know of a university graduate in philosophy named Paul Schlatter. One of Adolf Schlatter's great-grandmothers, Anna Barbara Zollikofer (1734–1818), was a direct descendant of Joachim Vadian (1484–1551), the Reformer of St. Gallen, whose statue can still be seen in the St. Gallen city center. Several ancestors on his grandmother's side served at the top of the city's citizenry as mayor.

Adolf Schlatter's grandmother, Anna Schlatter (1773–1826) née Bernet, earned a reputation extending far beyond the boundaries of St. Gallen. She cultivated an extensive correspondence with leading personalities of an influential movement known as the *Erweckung* ("Awakening"), a church-

1. Adolf Schlatter's grandmother, Anna Schlatter (1773–1826)

renewal movement that called for truly transformed hearts. This movement, especially in its early stages, transcended confessional boundaries in remarkable fashion. As a result, Anna Schlatter corresponded with quite an assortment of persons, including Lavater (1741–1801), Jung-Stilling (1740–1817), and Steinkopf (1773–1859). In addition, she was sought out by many well-known men and women of the time, including the Württemberg duchess Henriette and theologians such as F. D. E. Schleiermacher and M. de Wette. Her ecumenical broadness deserves special mention. She maintained close relations with the leading lights of the *Erweckung* in Catholic Bavaria, where about sixty priests were active in the movement. Among these were the "father" of the movement, the priest Martin Boos (1762–1825), along with his friend and benefactor, Johann Michael Sailer (1751–1832). Sailer, from the town of Landshut in Bavaria, was known for his peaceable and conciliatory spirit. He gained a reputation as a moral theologian and served as bishop of Regensburg.

Now it is true that at the beginning of the nineteenth century a certain openness prevailed toward believers of other confessions. This was one of the effects of the *Erweckung* movement, with its emphasis on truly transformed hearts independent of confessional affiliation. Still, it was by no means self-evident that Johann Michael Sailer would for a time spend his vacation with Catholic friends every two years in order to cultivate fellowship and spiritual exchange with Anna Schlatter and her sister, Judith. Anna Schlatter also had open contact with priests in St. Gallen and the surrounding area: the leading local Catholic pastor Haid visited her home from time to time, and she reciprocated—in those days a bold move!—by attending his worship services in the monastery chapel. She procured Bibles and the writings of Gerhard Tersteegen for other priests. It was inevitable that Anna Schlatter, just like her fatherly friend Lavater, would fall under suspicion of being a Catholic sympathizer. But she responded with conviction: "I recognize no middle wall of partition [cf. Eph. 2:14] and for my part do whatever I can to tear that wall down. Only faith and love make a Christian. The time will come when we are neither Catholic nor Reformed, of that I am certain; only Christ all in all." As we will see, in his own way Adolf Schlatter continued his grandmother's confessional openness—without in any way neglecting the necessity of serious theological struggle for the truth.

Adolf Schlatter

Anna Schlatter's varied contacts with luminaries of both Protestant and Catholic wings of the *Erweckung* are in themselves a remarkable testimony to her intellectual acuity and uncommon spiritual broadheartedness. One could point here to visits she made to Aloys Henhöfer (Mühlhausen), Christian Heinrich Zeller (Beuggen), Gottlieb Wilhelm Hoffmann (Korntal), and others. But these contacts are still more remarkable when one notes that this extraordinary woman's inter-

2. Theodor Zahn (1838–1933), New Testament and patristics scholar

3. Hektor Stephan Schlatter (1805–80), Adolf Schlatter's father

est did not result in neglect of her family. Rather, she was an exemplary wife and mother. With the aid of much prayer every one of her eleven children carried on the Christian heritage of their home in ways appropriate to them. The correlation of spiritual and natural productivity in the Schlatter tribe borders on the miraculous: of Anna Schlatter's more than nine hundred descendants that can be traced down to 1935, no fewer than sixty-six became theologians and six were missionaries!

Apart from Adolf Schlatter the most important of these theologians was Theodor Zahn (1838–1933), well-known for his New Testament commentaries and patristic scholarship. There was also the noted preacher and theological writer Adolf Zahn (1834–1900) as well as Berlin pastor Johannes Burckhardt (1853–1914). Burckhardt gained renown far beyond Berlin for various charitable activities, most of all in

4. Wilhelmine Schlatter (1819–94), née Steinmann, Adolf Schlatter's mother

the area of pastoral care for young women. He was also instrumental in construction of the *Versöhnungskirche* (Church of the Reconciliation) in Berlin.

Adolf Schlatter's father, Hektor Stephan Schlatter, was born in St. Gallen on November 13, 1805, the eleventh child of Anna Schlatter. His mother would have been glad to see him become a pastor. But a fear of spiritual office and a pronounced bent toward the natural sciences caused Stephan

5. The Schlatter family home, *Haus hinterm Turm*, in St. Gallen. Built in 1523.

Schlatter to train instead as a pharmacist. After a time of retreat from the Christian faith he found his way back to living faith in Christ, to the great joy of his mother, shortly before her death in 1826. On June 18, 1839, he married Wilhelmine Schlatter (1819–94) of St. Gallen. Five years earlier, at his father's urging, he had laid aside his work as a pharmacist to take over his parents' grocery store in the *Haus hinterm Turm* ("house behind the tower") directly adjacent to the Protestant parish church of St. Laurenzen.

It is no exaggeration to say that the marriage of Adolf Schlatter's parents, blessed with nine children, was unusually happy and satisfying. It left a deep impression on the children for their entire lives. For Adolf Schlatter's inner development one can hardly overestimate how significant this family background was. He grew up in a family that was not merely "intact"; rather, it was marked by a rich measure of convincing faith and deep love. In Schlatter's later years he repeatedly and effusively praised the basic positive experience he had enjoyed in his parents' home: "I will praise your priceless gift; I offer profound thanks, Lord, for my paradise. The boy enjoyed many a year of pure air. Home—your glow will never leave me."

In less poetic strains Schlatter summarized the quintessence of the enduring fruit of the nurture he had enjoyed: "In our home I had *seen* love." From parents "I received the Bible, prayer, Sunday, the clarification of what the words faith and love mean." His parents "lived out their lives before us and for our sakes and . . . I *saw* from the very start what a life lived in God's presence looks like. The power with which we children were embraced by our parents' faith was the presupposition and root from which my own history grew." When in his theology Schlatter later unfailingly emphasized the fundamental significance of "seeing" and "perceiving" for the rise of Christian faith, he was only drawing the theological consequences from the impression left by his parents' home. Perceiving a "life lived in God's presence" and "seeing" what "love" looked like showed him once for all that faith and love are not concepts alien to life. They are not unattainable demands. They are life-determining and therefore perceptible realities that confirm the message of the gospel everywhere that the call of Jesus is heeded. Schlatter's later insistence on the fruits of faith, on love and works, was the logical

6. Modern view of Schlatter family home in St. Gallen

outcome of his earliest years of childhood, during which his own faith arose in almost natural fashion with the aid of the faith that his parents lived out.

The childhood experience just sketched also explains why we will search in vain for a datable conversion in Schlatter's development. Trust in Jesus appears to have determined the life of Adolf Schlatter from early on. Born on August 16, 1852, as a seventh child (following two brothers and four sisters), he quite naturally found his place in the belief structures of his parents. In Schlatter's numerous later comments on his childhood and youth there is not so much as a hint that prior to university studies he ever saw faith in Jesus Christ as somehow problematic, or that he entertained rejecting it. Similar to the great Pietists Spener (1635–1705), Graf von Zinzendorf (1700–1760), and J. C. Blumhardt (1805–80), he experienced no "breakthrough" in his inner life that separated a faithless phase of life from a later time of belief. The first discernible profound upsurge in a mature faith was Schlatter's decision to pursue theological studies. He regarded this as so significant for his life that he could later describe it as a "conversion." But by this he did not mean a turn from godless living to following Jesus; he rather spoke of the willingness to allow himself to be claimed, in a binding and irrevocable sense, by full-time service to Christ and the community of believers.

It is by no means self-evident that Schlatter would so readily make the *Erweckung*-based spiritual world of his parents his own. The opposite is notoriously the case in numerous other examples of the children of pious parents. But Schlatter's (and his siblings') affirmation of the faith was facilitated by his parents' rare spiritual wisdom. They deftly related the spiritual and the natural, joy in God's creation and gratitude for Christ's redemption, in such a way that their children experienced, from a very early age, being a Christian as a pleasant opportunity rather than a stifling burden.

Schlatter's parents guided their children into a lifestyle closely bound to nature. Frequent outdoor treks and familiarity with indigenous animal and plant life awakened in young Adolf a deep joy in the glory of creation: "We children were . . . often out of doors, sometimes with our parents and sometimes alone, and enjoyed the Alps at a time when such mountain pastimes were not yet popular with others in our town. Many recollections of my youth glow with the brightness of that glorious landscape, through which we raced in every direction. My eyes, therefore, were opened to nature at an early age, for God had given me parents who praised him with earnest faith as the Creator of nature."

Adolf Schlatter's delight in nature, awakened at such an early age, stayed with him for his whole life. It was plainly visible in the lively naturalness that characterized all he did, a trait that later greatly aided students in arriving at a more joyous and less inhibited life of faith. It found expression most of all, however, in the unusually positive view of creation, an optimistic theological assessment of nature, which is a distinctive of Schlatter's theology. Later in life Schlatter laid great emphasis on the thesis that God's love and glory are revealed in the created order, not just in Jesus' incarnation and redemption. The roots of this conviction lie in the sense of the close inner connections between the natural and the spiritual that Schlatter's parents attempted to impart to their children.

The unity of creation and redemption, nature and grace, found symbolic expression in a certain room of Schlatter's boyhood home. This unique room, set aside for solitude, left an indelible impression: "In our home was a sort of private chapel containing unusual fixtures. It was a room that granted peace and privacy to anyone who sought it. It lay above our living quarters in the attic space, which also served as a storage area for lumber. . . . Father used it to give us an impression of the greatness of nature through a wide range of objects. Boxes hid physical instruments, an old electric device, and the like, as well as Father's large herbarium. The walls were lined with minerals and animals, whether mounted or in picture form. A few pictures of Bible scenes were a reminder of Scripture. Nature and Scripture together, it was thought, should speak to us as God's revelation. This all pointed to the foundation on which the whole life of our home was grounded."

Near the end of his life Schlatter confessed that he had never seen "anywhere a church or chapel . . . in whose ornamentation" the dual revelation of nature and Scripture received such "powerful expression" as in the quiet chapel-room of the home of his youth.

His boyhood home's close bond of the natural and the spiritual was a weighty factor in the young Schlatter's life and faith. For his family's "understanding of nature as God's creation was . . . not just a principle with no bearing on how we lived but rather thoroughly influenced all we did. The whole natural realm became a source of joy. We ate with joy, hiked with joy, and worked with joy."

In his book *Erlebtes* Schlatter comments that his parents' high regard for the gloriousness of nature, passed along to him and his siblings, was decisive for Schlatter's mature reflection. It helps explain why he made it the heartbeat of Christian faith, faith in the redemption that Jesus won. He writes, "I highly doubt that our parents' Christian convictions would have gripped and moved us as they did if they had denied us access to nature. When I ask myself why, after regular attendance at Sunday morning church, I would often attend the evening service at eight with my mother, without any coercion whatsoever, then the answer is clear: between the morning and evening service lay the afternoon with an enjoyable hike. Once we sat atop a hill with an especially striking view of beautiful Lake Constance before us. Father and my sisters struck up a hymn with the words, 'Even if we're just poor sinners, he loves us no less for that. O, he loves us dearly.' What made that credible? Before me lay the wide expanse of God's handiwork; and he who had placed it there for our eyes to feast on 'loves us dearly.' God remains incredible to us when no great work of his hands fills our sight, and the first work of God that it is our job to see is nature."

Such words underscore the fundamental importance of his parents' nature-oriented lifestyle, not only for Schlatter's character formation, but also for his spiritual development. They help explain why a decisive—and in twentieth-century theology quite unusual—affirmation of the natural realm, with significance for both dogmatics and ethics, lay at the center of Schlatter's later theological instruction.

Schlatter's theology of creation sometimes met with the objection that it was overly optimistic, that it did not take the "dark side" of nature with sufficient seriousness. To this Schlatter repeatedly responded that he had been quite familiar, from earliest youth, with the side of nature that produced suffering and death. In fact, nature was for him a greater hindrance to faith than history: "I recognize that [nature] is also our adversary, that it looms before us like a wall that obscures God from our view. My wounds of spiritual struggle have not come from consideration of history [but of nature]."

Already in childhood and youth Schlatter felt the "bitter severity" of nature: his oldest brother was severely handicapped, both mentally and physically. His younger brother, the family's ninth child, had been stillborn. His wonderfully gifted sister, Monika, died of typhoid fever at the age of nineteen, just after completing her education. Yet all these setbacks failed to thwart the grateful assessment of the natural order that reigned in the Schlatter household. Why? Because the parents convincingly modeled to their children a living faith in Jesus that centered on a hope that transcended, though did not denigrate, creation. Looking back Adolf Schlatter commended his parents' testimony by observing that they never succumbed to the temptation of "disparaging the natural order" or of accusing God, even in the face of sickness and death in their family. Their travail triggered "no cry for God to justify his ways, no shaking or sundering of faith because of pessimism's ravages." Instead, Schlatter writes, "Over their view of nature stood the words, 'The Lord gave, and the Lord has taken away; blessed be the name of the Lord' [Job 1:21]."

His parents' basic attitude became especially clear to Schlatter at the death of his sister Monika in 1865. "We children were called into the bedroom. We stood encircling the bed of our deceased sister. Then our parents accompanied us to the living room, where Bibles were opened and we read Revelation 21 and 22. Our sister was dead: the first gap torn in our little family circle. Our pain was profound. But instead of lament our parents placed before us that word which sheds a ray of light on God's ultimate purposes. They did not just look back on a lost past, nor again gaze questioningly into an unknown future, but rather set their gaze and ours on God's eternal city. I encountered the incomparable hope that the New Testament mediates. Such hope detaches us from our pain and personal possessions, situates our lives in God's grand scheme, and shows us our place as members of the great fellowship he creates, a fellowship that is eternal because it is God's."

No less influential on Schlatter as a child was his parents' handling of their handicapped child. Schlatter's oldest brother had serious mental, hearing, and speech limitations. Yet through his parents' faith and love these limitations became the source of a fruitful experience for the entire household. "Our abnormal brother's presence in our tightly knit family fellowship greatly enhanced that fellowship. 'What do you have that you did not receive?' [1 Cor. 4:7]. These words stood before us with a clarity that made them impossible to overlook."

Later in life Schlatter would lay strong emphasis on man as a being who is in every respect *dependent on what he receives*. All human potential is really a gift. This accent on reception is rooted decisively in the basic experience of having a handicapped brother. That this experience was felt as positive, however, by Schlatter and his siblings may be credited to the wonderful manner in which his parents handled the challenge that they faced: "They made the pain caused by the abnormal condition of their oldest son completely invisible. It goes without saying that he was protected from being treated disdainfully. But he was also not tortured with sympathy, nor did he receive the kind of love that makes the recipient aware that he is pitied. . . . Our brother had the full right to be what he was."

In summary it must be said that Schlatter was confronted with nature's "dark side" in a quite considerable measure from an early age. His parents' exemplary, creation-affirming faith protected him, however, from overlooking the "bright side" of creation with all that it grants and preserves. This parental guidance in perceiving the gloriousness of nature opened Schlatter's eyes to a fact too often overlooked: nature is not primarily "an institute whose purpose is to effect our death," but is rather "*first of all* the root of our lives" that graces us "daily with its inexhaustible treasure." This basic insight was stressed in Schlatter's theology of creation, an aspect of his outlook that never wavered throughout his whole career.

Adolf Schlatter owed his parents something more than the affirmation of God the Creator and his creation. He also witnessed their affirmation of faith in Jesus Christ and his redemption. So then, he received not only the basic principles of his doctrine of creation, but also the starting point of his doctrine of faith. His parents lived their lives before their children in such a way that the substance of Christian faith did not consist in mere assent to dogmatic truths or confessional convictions. It consisted rather in trusting heart devotion to Jesus Christ. Though the parents remained members of different Christian confessions, they took admirable steps to maintain unity in what is essential to the faith. Schlatter's father had helped found a free church in St. Gallen. It constituted formally in 1837 with a private observance of the Lord's Supper after initial formation in 1836 as a discussion group. He was rebaptized, like other members of this fellowship, in 1838 and thereby separated decisively from the Reformed church. He was deeply wounded, however, when his wife found it impossible to follow his example. She and all their children remained members of the Reformed church in St. Gallen. It left a lasting impression on Adolf Schlatter that the ecclesiastical separation of his parents, which often pained them greatly, could not destroy the deep bonds they shared in the faith and in love.

This experience became central to Schlatter's inner development and later theological formation. In his autobiography *Rückblick auf meine Lebensarbeit* (*Reflections on My Life's Work*) he writes, "Our parents succeeded in the fellowship of the faith despite their ecclesiastical rupture because their faith was grounded, not in the church, but in Jesus. . . . Jesus was shown to me as the decisive, ultimately determinative ground of faith." This insight had lasting effect on Schlatter's understanding of the faith. Later it preserved him from becoming a reactionary confessional theologian.

In theological and ecclesiastical spheres Schlatter continued the heritage of his mother. Yet he took serious measures to adopt the intelligible and justified spiritual concerns of his father. Chief among these were the correct observations that church discipline was lax and that lay participation in local church ministry was deficient. Schlatter later rigorously pursued the question of the boundaries and restrictions of the churches of the Reformation, or—to put it positively—inquired after the "fulfillment of the Reformation" in the sense of a deepened appropriation of Holy Scripture. But such queries had already been awakened under his parents' roof.

Schlatter's father made it easier for his son to take seriously the spiritual motives that moved him. For in an impressive way he sought to keep himself free from the dangers of separatistic piety. He forced neither his wife nor his children to follow his example but left them full freedom in this respect. He knew himself to be bound to all who sought seriously to be Christians, regardless of the confession to which they belonged. In locales other than St. Gallen he repeatedly attended worship services with his children to hear Reformed preachers whose message he valued. In spite of his reservations about the state church he took thorough pleasure in Adolf Schlatter's entrance into the ordained ministry in that church. In contrast to Baptist teaching of his day he refused to force his understanding of "believer's baptism" on Christians who upheld the biblical status of the doctrine of infant baptism. Rebaptism was not required in the free evangelical church of St. Gallen, in which he preached regularly until shortly before his death.

Stephan Schlatter was also well aware of the danger of spiritual arrogance, whether open or hidden, which often accompanies separation from a church. His basically ecumenical (in the good sense) posture received affirmation at his funeral (July 1880), attended not only by the leaders of the canton's free churches but also by pastors of the state church. Stephan Schlatter's life of faith was too sincere and upright to avoid winning the respect of even those Christians who disagreed with his separation from the state church. Adolf Schlatter's youngest sister, Dora, stated after her father's death that she rejoiced "to have had a father whom I could place alongside the Sermon on the Mount without embarrassment." Adolf Schlatter's autobiographical remarks on his boyhood home likewise reflect deep respect for his father's spiritual life.

By his frequent visits to the sick, his helping the needy, and his tireless work in Bible distribution (partially alone, partially through envoys, he distributed nearly one hundred thousand Bibles and New Testaments!), Stephan Schlatter was known and highly regarded far beyond his own church and the confines of St. Gallen. Church historian Wilhelm Hadorn justly describes him as "the most endearing and . . . sympathetic separatist . . . whom we encounter in the history of Pietism."

The effect of Adolf Schlatter's mother was more hidden from view but no less consistent and effective. She drew strength not only from the faith she shared with her husband, but also from regular worship attendance at the state church as well as daily evening devotions. Her religious influence on her children was not restricted to their remaining in the state church but extended to obvious deep impressions on their inner lives. Adolf Schlatter's retrospective comment on her role as a Christian mother speaks for itself: "Her worship took shape in the way that she managed her house. It showed the fruit of her inner life—well ordered, full of peace, clean, and pleasant. She was the living conscience of her children."

This woman, her labor hidden from public view, certainly could not foresee the outcome of her costly decision to guide her children into a vital relationship with Christ within the state church. She could not have imagined the great theological significance and immeasurable blessing for Christendom that would result, as her decision placed her son, Adolf, in a sphere of influence that would not have been open to him as a member of his father's small free evangelical church—assuming he would still have studied theology after separating from the state church. The high cost of her decision to remain in the state church over several decades is seen in an exchange with her daughter, Dora. Once Dora remarked to her aged mother, "Oh, Mom, how grateful we are that you kept us near the trunk of the great tree that is the church and didn't get us out on some shaky little branch." Her old mother's reply: "Yes, I'm sure you are. But it was very difficult, and I might do it differently if I had it to do over now!"

In light of all the above, it is clear that Adolf Schlatter received from his parents not only a vital faith in Jesus Christ but also a wealth of encouragement in both a spiritual and a natural sense. In later years this encouragement would prove extraordinarily fruitful for both his practical life and his theological achievement.

Yet, as in every childhood, it was not only the parental home that exerted lasting influence on Schlatter's later life. Along with his parents there were additional close relatives, especially Daniel Schlatter (1791–1870), a missionary to the Tartars, and Bible translator Gottlieb Schlatter (1809–87), who had an enduring effect. And then there was school. After four years of elementary school Schlatter advanced to the next level for three more years. On the basis of the high quality of his work ("I was . . . top in the class"), he entered the second class of the St. Gallen *Gymnasium* (advanced secondary school) in the spring of 1865. Although Schlatter's parents were determined to shield their family from everything "worldly" ("For us the theater, the dance hall, and the bars did not exist"), they were nevertheless committed to furnishing their children with an education corresponding to their gifts. Four of their five daughters were trained as teachers (at that time university education was not open to women), and two of their three sons attended the *Gymnasium*, necessary for subsequent college-level study.

The parents took pains to challenge their children intellectually in other respects, too. Not only Christian hymns "but also the whole gamut of German folk songs" were common fare in their family life. The artistic gifts of one daughter were zealously cultivated; the Schlatters regularly visited art exhibitions in St. Gallen. Adolf Schlatter speaks of "going from picture to picture, gazing on each with inner devotion." Nor were the parents stingy with reading material. True, their personal library apparently did not contain a huge number of books; Schlatter mentions their religious collection as consisting only of works by Johann Arndt, Martin Boos, John Bunyan, and Johann Kanrod Pfenniger. But Adolf Schlatter's thirst for knowledge could be fully slaked by means of the St. Gallen city library as well as a local theological library.

The *Gymnasium* opened up an intellectual world to Schlatter that was previously hidden. If his parents had used nature to train him in his "capacity to see," the *Gymnasium* equipped him with "the capacity to read, the historical sense." The *Gymnasium* that Schlatter attended was strong in the natural sciences. But the humanities disciplines were of even greater importance for the young Schlatter. He proved to have extraordinary gifts in classical Latin and Greek, so much so that his teacher gave him private lessons each Sunday forenoon from eleven to twelve. Later this same teacher would be better known as Dr. Misteli, linguist at the university in Basle.

Thus already prior to college-level study Adolf Schlatter acquired the essentials of his linguistic preparation. This equipped him for the philological precision that ranked among the chief features of his exegesis and New Testament interpretation throughout his life. Since Misteli guided him in the reading of entire books, Schlatter (while still in secondary school!) voluntarily read "Ovid, Virgil, and Homer, not just in excerpts, but in their entirety." At the same time he expended "much time" on other readings of his own selection, since he was not satisfied with the instruction he was receiving. This reading extended beyond ancient authors to include theological and philosophical works that were then current. For example, it was at this time that he first took up Kant.

Schlatter's encounter with school deeply influenced his inner development. From the start he felt a considerable tension between the religious and moral outlook of his parents' home and the reigning outlook at school: "At home Jesus' teachings were the norm. No one told lies, and there was no place for theatrics to call attention to oneself . . . ; we were bound to one another in implicit trust. At school, however, lying was common; school generated and required deception. At home no one harassed the other or sought to seize some advantaged position by means of selfish greed. Each cared for the other: Father for Mother, Mother for Father, our parents for us children—and we children obeyed our parents. At school everyone harassed everyone else; school comrades harassed both the teacher and each other. There was an utter lack of awareness of the meaning of the word love."

This rather negative sketch of school life shows the deep contrast that Schlatter felt between his home and school. Yet to stop here would give a quite misleading impression of Schlatter's overall experience there. If one surveys all of Schlatter's statements about that period in his life, a very different picture emerges. Thus his recollections about teachers are by no means primarily disparaging: "In my school days my teachers did me a great deal of good." In the case of his Greek teacher Misteli the amount of good was considerable indeed. But Schlatter saw that something vital was commonly lacking: the true teacher's knack for kindling students' curiosity and bringing out their capabilities. And most of all, he nowhere found the love that he was familiar with from his upbringing. One must ask here, of course, whether Schlatter's sharp criticism of his school days is not the result of applying an impossibly high standard, one that must necessarily cast a state-regulated school in an unfavorable light. In any case it would be unfair to conclude from his rather negative statements that his overall experience was unusually dismal. More gloomy features of his description must be understood in the light of the unusually favorable training that he enjoyed.

Of still greater significance for Schlatter in his secondary school years was his first encounter with liberal theology (embodied in a religion teacher) and the idealist philosophy of Hegel and Kant (to which two of his teachers were devoted). Theological liberalism and idealist philosophy were among the intellectual forces with which Schlatter the theologian interacted intensively his entire life. His first brush at school with these movements did little to convert him to their views. The instruction of his liberal religion teacher, "who had taken flight from parish ministry into the school," struck him as thoroughly "desolating," inasmuch as this teacher showed no trace of inner sympathy for the spiritual content of the New Testament. At most his concern extended to the New Testament's ethical teaching. This same teacher introduced him to idealist philosophy in the form of Hegel (1770–1831) near the end of Schlatter's secondary school training; the exposure raised red flags for Schlatter because of Hegel's onesidedly rationalist orientation. On the other hand, the philosophy of Kant (1724–1804), taught by Schlatter's Kant-loving language teacher Misteli, awakened sufficient interest that Schlatter read a few of Kant's works on his own. Yet these readings do not seem to have resulted in essential shaping of Schlatter's own outlook.

In any case Schlatter's contact with Hegel and Kant gave him his first impressions of German idealist philosophy. This philosophy would continue to demand his attention during university study. He wrestled with it, in fact, his entire life, for the relation of the biblical tradition to idealist philosophy turned out to be one of the basic questions animating Schlatter's theological work.

Schlatter's extraordinary linguistic aptitude and the scientific interest in linguistics spawned by his teacher Misteli nearly caused Schlatter to study philosophy rather than theology. To do so would have been to go against a long-standing secret desire of his mother. In a discussion with his oldest sister Schlatter justified his intention: "Theological study is dangerous and could easily shake one's faith." But the critical response of his sister convinced him that fleeing from theological study would be a truly cowardly and faithless course of action. Looking back Schlatter said, "I felt that if I avoided theological study out of fear I would not be preserving my faith but actually giving it up." The fateful decision to be willing to pursue theological study was of fundamental personal significance: "I see no comparable juncture in my life that had such decisive effect on my personal direction. I came to the conclusion that avoiding theological study to preserve faith was rank hypocrisy, and this conclusion brought decisive consequences. When people ask me to describe the day of my conversion, I am inclined to tell them that it was the day of my decision to study theology."

Schlatter later conceded that the anxiety over formal theological study that he felt as a youth was not without foundation, since it can indeed be detrimental to personal faith. But he also insisted that to act solely on the basis of this anxiety would not be to act "from faith" because it would fail to take account of the capacity of God's preserving grace.

In further preparation for his theological study, Schlatter learned Hebrew near the end of his secondary schooling. In the spring of 1871, having received his *Abitur* (advanced high school diploma), he left St. Gallen in order to take up theological study at the University of Basle.

2

College Days in Basle and Tübingen

Schlatter began his theological study with joy and "high hopes." The decision to pursue this course had not come easily, because he took quite seriously the dangers that interaction with critical theology could pose for his spiritual life. Now, however—in the wake of the discussion with his sister—he sallied forth confidently. He wanted to work his way "seriously into academic theological study." Yet he was still uncertain whether he should pursue a call to the pastorate after such study. A decision for vocational church service would depend on his later "religious position."

With voracious intellectual appetite and equally vigorous "joy in learning" Schlatter took up his studies. According to the prescribed curriculum, the main topic in the first semester was philosophy. On the train journey from St. Gallen to Basle (both in Switzerland) Schlatter encountered the pastoral counsel of his mother. "You will now study philosophy," she told him. "That is interesting for the person who has not yet come to faith. But for the believer such study gets to be burdensome and disgusting." Schlatter recalls his response: "Within me reverberated words like 'That's not true!' . . . I was . . . offended by the self-seeking narrowness of this judgment, which looked on something as attractive only if it brought me gain. Wasn't philosophy a significant aspect of the history of our people and of all humankind? Was it not for that reason worthy of painstaking attention, even if it brought no gain to me personally?"

This intellectual openness for authentic exposure to philosophy is characteristic of the four semesters Schlatter spent

7. Adolf Schlatter as student in Basle, 1871–73

8. Karl Steffensen (1816–88), Schlatter's philosophy professor in Basle

in Basle. For two years he sat attentively in the lecture hall of philosopher Karl Steffensen (1816–88), hearing his lectures on logic and the history of philosophy. The latter encompassed philosophical thought from antiquity to the "history and criticism of philosophical systems since Kant." In addition he heard lectures by the Aristotelian Rudolf Eucken on "scientific method" and "Aristotle's basic principles" in the winter semester of 1871–72. Schlatter's shorthand notes of these lectures, containing many Greek citations from Aristotle, can be seen today in the Schlatter archives in Stuttgart, Germany. Schlatter later expressed regret that due to time constraints he could not "follow Eucken seriously, who would have opened up the way to Aristotle for me. Here I unfortunately remained at the elementary level."

In the same semester lectures by Friedrich Nietzsche on Plato's Dialogues had a more enduring—though negative—impact: "The chief impression that I internalized from his lectures arose from his offensive haughtiness. He treated his listeners like despicable peons. He convinced me of the principle that to throw out love is to despoil the business of teaching—only genuine love can really educate."

In addition to the philosophy classes that comprised the lion's share of Schlatter's first four semesters at Basle, he also attended theological lectures by Old Testament scholars Hermann Schultz and Emil Kautzsch, New Testament scholar Hermann Freiherr von der Goltz, and church historian Karl Rudolf Hagenbach. At the same time, from the very first semester he devoted himself to the study of Arabic and Hebrew under the Arabic specialist Socin. He also studied history under the renowned historian Jakob Burckhardt, whose lectures he digested "with raptest attention."

It becomes obvious that Schlatter threw himself into the questions posed by philosophy and theology without reservation. His first semesters are free from the kind of anxiety that is intent only on the preservation and confirmation of the faith that one already possesses. Schlatter was thoroughly willing to put the faith of his upbringing with its roots in the *Erweckung* (Awakening) to the critical test. He took pains, however—at least at first—to keep his faith in Jesus separate from academic cross-examination. At that time he held the conviction, which he would later vigorously dispute, that the touchstone of Christian faith—personal relationship to Jesus through trust in him—is totally independent of scientific knowledge and therefore can neither be placed in question nor confirmed by scientific criticism. Therefore, he reasoned, there is no danger to faith in subjecting the Christian tradition to limitless criticism. In a letter of June 6, 1871 he wrote to his mother, who had become concerned, "Don't trouble yourself about the course that my inner development will take," because the question of belief or disbelief is not a scientific but a practical question, which "has no direct connection to scientific work." On the other hand, the church's teaching, passed down through the centuries (and the content of the faith professed by the *Erweckung*!) is dependent on science and is "*not* an authority for the onward march of [scientific] research."

It is understandable that Schlatter's mother was concerned for the spiritual development of her son as she sensed him beginning to strike out in his own direction. Her cares no doubt intensified as Schlatter defied her wish that he join a youth group in Basle whose members embraced *Erweckung*-type beliefs. The striking reason he gave was that the group members were "foreign" to the things that currently moved Schlatter. Instead Schlatter attached himself to the student association *Schwizer-hüsli*, a group with a Christian orientation whose goals resembled those set by Wingolf. Some two decades before the older Friedrich Bodelschwingh (1831–1910) had belonged to this same association. Here Schlatter found what was lacking in the *Erweckung*-group commended by his mother: intensive intellectual exchange on a Christian basis with students from different faculties in an atmosphere of freedom.

Schlatter threw himself zealously into the *Schwizer-hüsli* from the beginning. He took joy in the personal fellowship of the other members, in the hikes they took together, and especially in the discussions on scientific issues that took the form of lectures given by various members of the group in turn. Here Schlatter had the opportunity to give his first scientific paper (the manuscript is extant). It dealt with the question that was of particular importance to him in his first semester: the relation between faith and scientific research. Schlatter attempted to bring more clarity to this issue by reflecting on Augustine's treatise "De ultilitate credendi." His ongoing experience, however, inclined in the direction, seen in the letter to his mother, of the radical separation of scientific knowledge and faith.

In the first semester it appears that Schlatter's radical openness to scientific criticism posed no threat to his Christian faith. He continued regular church attendance and Bible reading. But in the second semester he plunged into the grip of a crisis of faith: on December 24, 1871, he wrote his parents asking them to pray for him. "Dear Parents, keep my situation always before you. . . . This semester appears to be a rather important one for me, taking me through a *tremendous inner crisis*. . . . May the Lord grant me, quite soon, the bright light of untroubled faith, the light that comes precisely to those . . . who languish in darkness."

The crisis mentioned tersely in this letter is certainly the critical phase in his formal studies about which he wrote decades later in his autobiography *Rückblick auf meine Lebensarbeit* (*Reflections on My Life's Work*). He tells how he "pored over Spinoza until late in the night with passionate zeal to see if I had it in me to become a Spinozan instead of a Christian." It was apparently in that semester that his philosophy professor Steffensen treated the Jewish philosopher Baruch Spinoza, who expressly rejected the Jewish-Christian conception of a personal Creator-God, replacing it with a pantheistic understanding of reality.

Schlatter's crisis reached to the foundations of his faith in Christ and in God and brought him to the point, at least for a time, of seriously doubting God's existence. "I can still point to the place in Basle where, as I walked to the college, I came near to making the blasphemous demand, 'If you exist, God, then show yourself to me.'" In that second semester Schlatter was obviously questioning not merely the *Erweckung-*

faith of his parents, as during the first semester, but the Christian faith as a whole!

Schlatter weathered the crisis "without being able to name a particular event that could have brought about a sudden change." According to Schlatter's own testimony, however, a decisive factor in persevering was steady exposure to Holy Scripture. In addition there were the important factors of his parents' abiding example and intercession, both of which Schlatter valued highly. Letters from Schlatter's student days show that for all his independence of thought and lifestyle, he never forsook his trust in and esteem for his parents. Thus he could write to his father, even during the midst of his "crisis semester," "You stand before the eyes of us, your children, as a shining example and highly visible guide through life" (November 11, 1871). Even if his parents could not help him with his intellectual doubts, they remained a positive force through their convicting practical Christian life. Their son could not easily discount the truth they exemplified when his hour of testing came.

By the summer semester of 1872 Schlatter appears to have overcome his faith crisis. He was uplifted by a burgeoning joy in the study of theology. "Day by day theological study grew more and more dear. Eventually I had . . . to institute definite measures so that my philosophical studies did not suffer neglect by comparison" (May 25, 1872). On the other hand, his appreciation grew for the instruction of his philosopher professor Steffensen, who had captured his fancy from the very first semester, counting himself now "among his students . . . always." Schlatter also wrote, "The man is worth his weight in gold."

In the fourth semester Schlatter finally finished off his philosophical studies with the compulsory comprehensive exams. Two years of intensive study had equipped him with the expertise that would later be indispensable for lectures in the history of philosophy that he delivered at Tübingen in 1905–6 and again in 1908. The focus of his studies and interest lay in contemporary philosophy, in particular, philosophical idealism. He could thank his first two years of university studies for extensive familiarity with that great stream of thought that he had first encountered in the *Gymnasium* and that he would not be able to escape throughout the whole of his career. For Protestant theology of the nineteenth and early twentieth centuries was dominated to a considerable degree by appropriation of, and sometimes reaction against, German idealism.

It was Steffensen's lectures that left the most enduring impression on Schlatter. This points to Schlatter's interest, not only in philosophy, but also in history: "I learned back then, and never forgot the lesson, that ideas, too, have their history. Through this history new formations arise from the old. . . . Steffensen helped me see through the notion of 'pure reason,' since his lectures brought to light the historical processes through which it arose."

All his life Schlatter attempted to apply this insight into the historically conditioned nature of reason, both in the realm of philosophy and in the realm of theology. He did this by paying attention, not only to philosophical or theological ideas as such, but also by noting their historical origins and consequences. Schlatter was convinced that whether in New Testament research or in the history of theology and philosophy, the "act of thinking" arises from the "act of living." The former cannot be regarded in abstraction from the latter.

It was not only the content of Steffensen's lectures that marked Schlatter deeply. It was also the seriousness he exuded as he treated the work of thinking as "a holy service." On the other hand, Steffensen's own philosophy failed to satisfy Schlatter: "We listened eagerly; for two years I listened attentively. But eager listening grows tiring, if what one hears is always just the question, but the answer is never forthcoming." Steffensen passed on to the young Schlatter, then, a good deal of knowledge about the history of philosophy along with valuable insight of abiding significance. But he failed to make

9. Tübingen, Germany (1907)

10. View of Tübingen from the Neckar River (1901)

a disciple out of his student. As Schlatter put it, "I took leave of my philosophical mentor—though with gratitude. I had witnessed a thinking person in action, a sight that many never see, a sight that is unforgettable for those privileged to experience it. But I saw something else, too: Ideas are not attained through the act of thinking alone."

In the summer semester of 1873 Schlatter switched his place of study to the southwest German city of Tübingen. He had considered going to Leipzig, presumably because of the

11. Johann Tobias Beck (1804–78)

renowned theologians Franz Delitzsch and Christoph Ernst Luthardt. He had also considered a semester of independent research in St. Gallen, since university regimentation made him long for the opportunity for self-directed study. But he decided, along with two Swiss comrades from the *Schwizer-hüsli*, to head for the university at Tübingen. One of his Swiss friends was Adolf Bolliger (1854–1931), who later taught philosophy, New Testament, dogmatics, and ethics at Basle.

Schlatter made the move in order to devote himself fully to the study of theology, for he had found the University of Basle unsatisfactory in this regard. True, the mediating theology of Schultz had made a good impression in his first two semesters. But overall the Basle theologians were even less convincing to Schlatter than the Basle philosophers. Once Schlatter had, in his first semester, distanced himself from the biblicistic-*Erweckung* theology of his parents, he sought in vain a satisfactory theological alternative. The so-called positive theology of the time, with its concern to preserve the authority of Scripture, did not convince him, although Schlatter took seriously its best proponents.

This indicates that he went to Tübingen because he hoped to receive additional clarification from the biblicist theologian Johann Tobias Beck (1804–78) who was teaching there at the time. Further evidence for this is the fact that as early as 1871 Schlatter had requested a volume of Beck's sermons from his parents, while in February 1872 he announced in a letter his interest in studying under Beck.

Schlatter arrived in Tübingen on April 17, 1873. His first impression of the city on the Neckar River was clearly one of disappointment. But he became so much at home "in this miserable dump called Tübingen" (April 18, 1873) that by the end of the same year he expressed gratitude that his path had led him into "my dear Tübingen" (December 31, 1873).

Behind this gratitude stands his encounter with Beck, who apparently far exceeded his expectations, making an impression that fairly bowled him over. Letters preserved from

Schlatter's student days reveal an almost gushing enthusiasm for Beck—in contrast to the much more reserved assessment contained in his autobiographical reminiscences of later years. As a student Schlatter depicted the famous professor as "an old, stooped, wizened little man" who spoke with "spiritual power." His lectures were spiritually penetrating, even causing "heart pounding" reactions in listeners (June 1, 1873). At first it was likely most of all Beck's personal and spiritual aura that fascinated the young Schlatter. At the end of his stint at Tübingen Schlatter offered the following reflection: "Tübingen brought me the great gain of placing before me a man who compelled my deepest regard and respect . . . a saintly original, a man who was spiritually one-of-a-kind, to the extent that we can even speak of anything on earth so clearly reflecting heaven" (August 16, 1874).

For the first time Schlatter encountered a theology professor whose spiritual existence and scientific work he sensed to be an uncontrived unity: "In the lecture hall he was confessor and researcher simultaneously. . . . He spoke therefore of God not as an absentee; he rather resembled Paul in speaking as one who was subject to Christ 'before God.' For me as for many others it was a tremendous experience to find myself in a classroom where what was honored was not godlessness as the precondition for being scientific. We rather found ourselves being addressed by a man moved by God."

Beck's effect on Schlatter was both pastoral and theological in nature. Schlatter felt personally addressed by Beck's "thunderous denunciation of casual study" and of neglecting "the simplest truths of conscience." As a result Schlatter, hoping "for an internal boost," decided "to let unnecessary externals occupy [him]" as little as possible in order to facilitate concentrated study and, at the same time, growth in the inner man (June 1, 1873).

Schlatter was greatly surprised to find that Beck, on a theologically reflective level, confirmed the simple biblical piety that reigned in his parents' home: "The old words of Scripture, familiar to one's ear from earliest childhood days . . . gain new life as Beck deals with them" (June 1, 1873). Beck knew how to pass on to the young student a new trust in Holy Scripture as reliable norm for all theological thinking: "I felt I was placed on the solid ground of eternal truth. . . . And the whole secret lies just here: that Beck had a knack for replicating on its own terms the entirety of scriptural truth . . . with extremely powerful liveliness" (June 20, 1873).

Schlatter's new trust in the authority of the Bible, kindled by Beck, never left him afterwards. His entire later theological research and teaching activity ultimately served to point in a scientifically grounded fashion to the normative importance of Scripture for life and teaching in the church. Schlatter championed Scripture's abiding challenge to the ecclesiastical setting that stands in constant danger of drifting away from the witness of Scripture.

Beck also brought Schlatter to a decisive awareness of the very great extent to which Holy Scripture frees theological thought from false alternatives: "It is amazing how many contradictions have been proposed which Scripture presents in dynamic relation: law and gospel, justification and sanctification, grace and wrath, revelation and reason, faith and understanding, etc. . . . Instead of contradictions Beck pursues the inner connections in which Scripture itself places each member of these pairs. Many a theological miscarriage collapses in its nothingness" (July 20, 1873).

From Beck Schlatter learned that fidelity to the truth of Scripture need not—as liberal thought of the time feared—improperly restrict or even do violence to theological reflection. Rightly understood such fidelity is necessary to liberate reason for satisfactory theological knowledge. This can take place where the whole scope of Scripture's truth is kept in view and where the individual components making up this truth are subordinated to the whole in a knowledgeable way. Beck inspired Schlatter to think in terms of overall unity, based on the inner agreement of the truths of Scripture. Such thinking links apparent theological alternatives with each other and shows their deeper unity. Schlatter's later theology would, like Beck's, be characterized by the positive mutual ordering of law *and* gospel, justification *and* sanctification, grace *and* wrath, revelation *and* reason, faith *and* understanding. And Schlatter's lifelong efforts later served to establish that the informed appropriation of the truth of Scripture (as opposed to mindless repetition) does not impair theological knowledge but rather enables and enhances it.

Beck was not Schlatter's only professor at Tübingen. He sat, for example, under the learned mediating theologian Landerer as he lectured on the creeds and confessions. He heard von Weizsäcker on the history of dogma and Roth on non-Christian religions—the latter because Schlatter saw in the history of religion a great demonstration of that "seeking and groping" of the heathen for God that is described in Acts 17:27 (May 2, 1873).

Along with extensive attention to Beck's theology, however, Schlatter also devoted special attention to Martin Luther during his Tübingen days. This study preserved Schlatter from following uncritically Beck's criticism of the Reformation. Schlatter was receptive to Beck's concern on this score, a concern that was familiar to Schlatter from his own parents' outlook. Yet he could not follow Beck in his questioning of the Lutheran doctrine of justification. Nor could Schlatter accept Beck's understanding of the relation between faith and history: Beck's ahistorical reproduction of the truths of Scripture stands in fundamental contradistinction from Schlatter's later concern to show the truths of the Bible in their concrete historical Sitz im Leben.

In summary, it can be said that Schlatter's Tübingen time was rich and filling. In an autobiographical statement filed after completing his studies, Schlatter wrote in an application for a clergy appointment that Tübingen was "incomparably more important" for his "religious and theological development than the time spent in Basle."

Adolf Schlatter

After three semesters Schlatter left Tübingen, which "had become so dear" to him (August 16, 1874), in order to finish up his studies back in Basle. In spite of his joy in academic work, a strong desire for practical church service had awakened in him since the winter semester of 1873–74. This had something to do with a peculiar disappointment that had descended on him: in spite of the various impulses from Beck he was not able to appropriate Beck's basic starting point because of its ahistorical quality. Not even in Beck did Schlatter find a theological mentor whom he was able to follow as a disciple, despite having gleaned so many exciting pointers from him. And so it happened that Schlatter completed his theological examinations in the spring of 1875 without having declared allegiance to any of the theological schools of the time or attaching himself to a loner like Beck.

On the basis of outstanding examination scores—he received the highest possible score (*sehr gut*) in every subject, commanding the respect of such examiners as the renowned liberal dogmatician Alois Emanuel Biedermann—the Basle professor Johannes Riggenbach invited him "to pursue doctoral studies." "A sufficient living allowance" for this was part of the invitation. But Schlatter turned down this attractive offer so that he could devote himself to ecclesiastical service instead. He made application "with apprehension" in view of his "personal weakness, immaturity, and lack of ability." Yet at the same time he was filled with joyful decisiveness, moved by the realization that the greater part of his countrymen were drifting away from any Christian moorings. For Schlatter this made it urgently necessary "to work with all seriousness and holy love to the end that the evangelical means of salvation be preserved among our people, and to work in such a way that this labor becomes the joy of my life."

3

Church Work in Kilchberg, Neumünster, and Kesswil

Schlatter's ecclesiastical service began with interim oversight of the pastoral office at Kilchberg on Lake Zurich. He received this assignment "in the middle of being interviewed by the supervisory pastor in Zurich." The church had earlier lost its pastor. Schlatter's task was to assume leadership until a permanent replacement could be found. After being ordained on the Sunday before Pentecost in 1875 at the St. Laurenzen Church in St. Gallen, he assumed his responsibilities at the age of twenty-three with considerable misgivings. The anxious feelings churning within him are captured in a poem he penned as an old man looking back on life:

High on a mountainside languished a church.
Upwards to it stretched my way.
Behind me lay . . . just student days.

Adolf Schlatter

Could I rise to the challenge ahead?
Burdensome pressure, grim load on my mind.
Slowly I trudged—and what would I find?

What is your goal, your intent, your desire?
Is preaching dry toil soon tasteless and drear?
Hark! Comes an answer: Jesus' own prayer,
Bolt from above, flame flashing forth hope.
"Father in heaven, hallowed be Thy name."
Away with all fear! My strength be his fame.

Those days but a memory, my life near its end—
Yet Jesus' request still sheds light on my way.
What more can I ask, what comfort request,
Than that selfsame plea with which I began.
"Father in heaven, hallowed be Thy name"—
Forever the source of my hope will remain.

In his various written reminiscences Schlatter passes on nothing more regarding his Kilchberg experience. But the depressing feeling of being overwhelmed at the beginning of his official church responsibilities, and overcoming the struggle by appropriating the Lord's Prayer anew, left an impression on him for the rest of his life. "Father, hallowed be Thy name" became a light to his path not only at Kilchberg but for all his subsequent activity as pastor and theology professor.

Schlatter worked in Kilchberg only three months. In August 1875 he was called to serve the congregation at Neumünster on the eastern shore of Lake Zurich. The pastor, a theological liberal by the name of Hiestand, asked Schlatter to come as his interim assistant. The idea was for Schlatter to satisfy that part of the congregation that wished to hear positive-biblical preaching, since their liberal pastor sounded quite different notes. The congregational situation was in some respects extremely delicate: "The part of the congregation that had distanced itself from the church [due to the liberalism of the head

58

12. Adolf Schlatter served in the pastorate from 1875 to 1880.

pastor and other scandals; see below] had taken violent measures that jeopardized the very existence of the pastoral office and the continuance of religious instruction in the schools. The congregation wanted to do away with one of the two established pastoral positions, in spite of the fact that the parish contained 16,000 members. Just the religious instruction of the youth was a giant task, because the school authorities had arbitrarily banned religious instruction from taking place during school hours and in school facilities." If internal congregational dissent was one danger, another came from the outside in the form of sorry circumstances that threatened support for the pastoral office even more: "There was a theology professor who entered the pulpit drunk; an education director who would occasionally be found passed out on the street; a congregational leader who had amassed considerable power for himself, who publicly stated that he made use of local houses of prostitution, yet was confirmed in his church office by a raucous majority."

Schlatter saw in Hiestand's request a task that he could not sidestep in view of the depressing state of the congregation. This would be, after all, an opportunity to push back the burgeoning de-Christianizing of the populace. When Schlatter applied for church office he had described his calling in terms of overcoming this rampant secularization. Here was his chance. Many years later Schlatter depicted the assignment that he "blindly" assumed as "much too difficult"—quite understandable given his age and relatively short time in office (August 1875–December 1876). Yet his effort was not fruitless. During Schlatter's year and a half of preaching and other duties at Neumünster, church attendance grew visibly. The existence of the disputed second pastoral position was assured by a vote in favor of a second clergyman, pending only a probationary period in office. At the end of 1876 Schlatter was able to take his leave of the situation "with a good conscience."

Schlatter's time in Neumünster was of abiding significance for him in several respects. In working alongside Hiestand he had his first direct contact with liberalism as an ecclesiastical reform movement. He had already encountered liberal theology in his studies. Especially in the winter semester of 1874–75, under the tutelage of Professor J. Riggenbach, he had interacted extensively with the liberal Swiss theologian Biedermann, a leading thinker of the time. Yet he had not yet faced the reality of liberal church practice. It was by no means self-evident that Schlatter, with his sympathy for positive-biblical theology in the wake of his studies under J. T. Beck, would consent to joint labor with a liberal colleague. Elsewhere in Basle at the time shared ministries between "positively" and "liberally" inclined clergy did not exist. In declaring himself willing to work with Hiestand for the sake of the congregation, Schlatter overstepped the principles that reigned in the home in which he grew up, principles that called for absenting oneself from worship services led by liberal clergy.

It can be said that Schlatter's work with Hiestand "succeeded . . . to a certain extent." The two quite differently oriented pastors achieved their mutual goals not through silence and skirting their differences but "through seizing every opportunity to air openly the convictions that separated [them]." The encounter with the liberal piety and church practice embodied in Hiestand was sobering for Schlatter. His impression was that liberal convictions "do not admit of popularization," since they stood "in diametrical opposition" not only to church tradition but also "to the reality of human life." In Schlatter's view the outcome of liberalism's opposition to church tradition was that liberal preaching became "void of content." On the one hand, it had to conceal its opposition to the substance of faith as understood in the church through the centuries. On the other, it lacked sufficient resources of its own to enable robust proclamation of the church's faith as now understood based on liberal premises. Schlatter felt that the result was helplessness in the pulpit and meaningless rhetoric in sermons. But the problems posed by liberalism's deficiencies were not going to be solved, in Schlatter's view, by "positives" and "liberals" refusing to work together. For the sake of the church, its members, and, most important, God, shared work was imperative for pastors of such very different orientations as Hiestand and Schlatter.

Of far-reaching effect in Schlatter's life ahead was his encounter with Edmund Fröhlich, "pastor at St. Anna (Zurich), site of a free-church preaching mission." A deep friendship arose between the two. On the Swiss National Day of Prayer in 1875 Fröhlich visited the worship service that

Adolf Schlatter

13. Schlatter's close friend, Edmund Fröhlich

Schlatter conducted and spontaneously decided to invite him to preach for his little congregation at St. Anna. Schlatter accepted the invitation, though a church official warned him that in doing so he would damage his "career." Looking back Schlatter recalls, "I laughed him to scorn. Career! In my youthful inexperience I had not yet run up against this tawdry concern." Apparently the existence of the St. Anna congregation, with its special status as free-church preaching mission supported by the pietistically inclined Evangelische Gesellschaft (Protestant Society), had its detractors in the Swiss canton of Zurich.

After preaching at St. Anna Schlatter "visited Fröhlich's home often." Fröhlich was a fascinating person at both the intellectual and spiritual levels. Apart from artistic giftedness he "carried on a fruitful pastoral ministry with appropriate and contagious earnestness, waging war against evil tirelessly in preaching and counseling. Yet at the same time he was a source of joy, dispensing cheer with his sunny disposition."

Schlatter was impressed by Fröhlich's insights into how to integrate pastoral activity with ongoing theological labor. Shortly before his first meeting with Fröhlich, Schlatter had penned a letter to his friend, Adolf Bolliger, in which he lamented the difficulty of sustaining theological reflection while fulfilling pastoral duties. But in Fröhlich he met a pastor who not only admonished him to theological growth ("You'll dry up," Fröhlich told Schlatter, "if you don't keep thinking") but showed by his own example "how to achieve this goal." Apparently Fröhlich had uncanny insight into how to avoid "the corruption of mindless pastoral activity," since he subjected his own pastoral work to a steady regimen of theological and philosophical readings, thus placing all he did on a theologically responsible foundation.

Fröhlich was deeply affected by the important Catholic lay theologian and philosopher Franz von Baader (1765–1841) and Baader's teacher St. Martin (1743–1803). Schlatter, at the urging of his new friend, digested their writings. The encounter with Baader turned out to be key for Schlatter. In him Schlatter found the thinker he had sought in vain during his student years, a "sure-footed theologian" who exerted enduring influence on Schlatter in both doctrinal and philosophical questions: "The fruit that familiarity with Baader brought me was not only the fearless joy of thinking that was implanted, never to depart. Most important of all was the help that his conceptual presentation of love turned out to be. All formulas then being used in the doctrinal teaching of our theologians to describe how love was demonstrated—cult, sacrifice, forgiveness, humility, service, fellowship—remained obscure and empty, while for Baader they possessed content and basis."

In the ensuing months Schlatter made Baader the subject of intensive study. Voluminous personal notes that still exist today in Schlatter's personal papers show that Schlatter worked through at least half of Baader's collected works, which fill sixteen volumes. He seems to have been particularly impressed and affected in the area of epistemology, in his assessment of German idealism, and in basic dogmatic and ethical questions. Schlatter received valuable impetus from Baader especially in the area of social ethics, for Baader was a pioneer in novel social-ethical theory then spreading

14. Pastor's house in Kesswil. Psychologist C. G. Jung, whose father was a pastor, was born in the same house just a few years earlier (1875).

in Catholic circles. In fact, he was one of the first—prior to Marx and Engels!—clearly to see the urgency of the social dimension of the Christian gospel and the need to address the plight of the burgeoning working class.

In January 1877 Schlatter followed a call to the congregation at Kesswil-Uttwil on Lake Constance. The three years he spent there were among the most pleasant of his life, "filled with what is most charming, fulfilling, and spiritually enriching in pastoral work. We enjoyed the natural happiness that the pastoral office can afford." In Kesswil Schlatter lived in a "beautiful manse in a lovely setting." The house can still be seen today. Just a year and a half before Schlatter moved there, the famous psychologist and pastor's son Carl Gustav Jung (1875–1961) was born to his predecessor in that same house. Schlatter was responsible for three village congregations, which involved preaching in two churches each Sunday. Church life there appears to have been lively, and Schlatter carried out his duties with great joy.

In Dozwil, the site of one of Schlatter's three congregations, he met the twenty-one-year-old daughter of a businessman. Her name was Susanna Schoop. Feeling "lonely" in the large manse, Schlatter wasted no time in pursuing marriage plans. "Deciding quickly" he courted her; they were engaged before the end of 1877 and married on January 15, 1878. Edmund Fröhlich preached at the wedding ceremony. Susanna Schoop proved to be a loyal mate, later following Schlatter willingly into the German academic world that was totally strange to her. Her painfully early death would snatch her from him on July 9, 1907. Schlatter never remarried.

Schlatter's letters to his bride and later wife have not yet been adequately assessed. But it can be said with certainty that they enjoyed a happy marriage. After her death Schlatter stated that their marriage was a felicitous fulfillment of the biblical text used at their wedding: "Love never fails" (1 Cor. 13:8).

15. Adolf and Susanna Schlatter as young marrieds

Schlatter was a shepherd to his congregations with heart and soul. It is likely that he would have remained a pastor for life if it had not been for a group of Pietists in the church at Bern who in 1880 asked that he take steps to qualify for a university post on the theological faculty there. This circle of Pietists was unwilling to continue putting up with a situation in which there had been not even a single positive-biblical theologian on the Bern faculty for two decades. The prevailing mood was, on the contrary, totally dominated by liberalism. They therefore undertook to encourage biblically oriented theologians to pursue an academic future by acquiring the necessary credentials to lecture in the university. The Pietists gained their first victory in 1878 when Old Testament scholar Samuel Oettli (1846–1911), whose views resembled their own, became associate professor of Old Testament. But Oettli found his position unsatisfactory without a like-minded colleague. So in the first weeks of 1880 he surprised Schlatter with a visit, hoping to sell him on the idea of joint work on the Bern faculty. Oettli expressed concern that "the result of his work would remain negligible if students were encouraged in their faith in Jesus only in their Old Testament classes." He told the astonished Schlatter, "You simply have to come!"

At first Schlatter had little inclination to consider Oettli's proposal. True, a year earlier he had thought about writing a doctoral dissertation on the biblical concept of law, going so far as to begin actual composition of the work he had in mind. But he finally abandoned these preparations and determined to devote himself to pastoral work. For that matter, even before Oettli's overtures Schlatter's friend Adolf Bolliger had repeatedly written letters pressuring Schlatter to take up doctoral work. But the pleas fell on deaf ears. It is no wonder that Schlatter was slow to respond to Oettli at first. But in their Kesswil discussion Oettli would not let the matter rest, pressing Schlatter until he agreed to examine the matter seriously and to get in contact with certain parties who would be willing to support him in his attempt.

During the final days of February 1880, Schlatter traveled to Bern to take a look at the situation for himself. On the way he spent time with his friend, Edmund Fröhlich, to solicit his counsel. Fröhlich advised Schlatter to accept the call.

Schlatter's first meeting with the Bern Pietists, on the evening of February 26, 1880, involved a great deal more difficulty than expected. First, Schlatter had to come to terms with the group of men who were in charge of two non-state Protestant schools in Bern: the Lerber School and Muristalden

Teachers' College. What these men, along with the other Pietists, had in mind was this: along with teaching at the university Schlatter would teach religion and Hebrew at their two schools. In this way his income would be assured. Since at first he would receive no state payment for his teaching activities in the university, a private association would have to be founded (the *Evangelische-kirchliche Verein*, or Protestant-Church Association). By drawing on this private source, Schlatter could be assured of a living wage, which would then be supplemented by whatever he could earn from university teaching. But before employment as a teacher Schlatter would have to submit to examination by the leaders of Lerber School and Muristalden Teachers' College. They would have to determine whether his views were sufficiently biblical.

The Lerber School director was Theoderich von Lerber (1823–1901), a committed fundamentalist. He roundly mistrusted Schlatter with his Swiss university theological training. Lerber's professed aim was to keep his school free from every form of biblical criticism. Schlatter could sense this mistrust. The first question he faced was: "Do you believe in the devil?" Other questions dealt with his views on the Virgin birth, the inspiration of Scripture, and other fundamental doctrines. Finally, he was asked about his personal faith. In response Schlatter recited the second article of Luther's Shorter Catechism question regarding the Apostles' Creed: "I believe that Jesus Christ, true God born of the Father from eternity and also true man born of the virgin Mary, is my Lord, who redeemed me, a lost and condemned creature, bought and rescued me from all sins, not with gold or silver but with his holy and precious blood and his guiltless suffering and dying; so that I might belong to him and dwell with him in his kingdom and serve him in eternal righteousness, innocence, and blessedness, just as he rose from the dead and lives and reigns for eternity. This is most certainly true."

Schlatter would always be thankful that in that moving moment he did not describe his "own relationship to Jesus" but made his personal confession "the general confession of Protestant Christendom" using terms that "Christendom has appropriated everywhere at all times." It was important to him to unite the personal and the general, the subjective and the objective, in this way.

Director Lerber's suspicions were not allayed, however, because Schlatter's remarks on the inspiration of Scripture seemed to him to fall short. This meant that Schlatter's employment was in grave danger, for Lerber could not give his consent. Others in the meeting that evening, however, took Schlatter's side and defended his explanation of the doctrine of inspiration against Lerber. In this discussion Schlatter kept silent for the most part. After spirited debate Lerber left the room. No agreement had been reached.

Schlatter returned home certain that the matter was dead in the water. "It will come to nothing," he told his wife. But to his astonishment he received word the next day from Lerber that nothing blocked his teaching in the two independent schools, since Lerber's "concerns and cares" had been "*fully* laid to rest" by Schlatter's remarks of the previous day. It was true, Lerber wrote, that he and Schlatter "had totally different starting points," but they both occupied "the identical ground of childlike and humble veneration of the divine word." Schlatter's patience, "inner warmth," and "profound seriousness" convinced Lerber "that we can work together fruitfully." Schlatter did not hesitate to relocate to Bern, although it was by no means clear whether and how he would be able to achieve faculty rank at the university there.

The move to Bern was a daring step of faith. There was no guarantee that his attempt to write an acceptable doctoral dissertation and receive faculty status would meet with success. But it was also a painful sacrifice, since Schlatter had discharged his pastoral duties with much joy and love: "Giving up my pastorate . . . was costly for me personally. A sign of how important it was to my life was the powerful longing

I felt to return to it. This desire was active for quite a long time."

For Schlatter's future course of action it was of great importance that his move into academic teaching was not one he had chosen for himself. Nor was it a flight from church ministry. He rather felt himself called by professing believers to this work: "From the very start—even as a mere instructor—I knew myself to be called to teach, and not just by an administration or faculty. I was called by parents who desired theological instruction for their children, by church supporters who demanded theology that would nourish the church. When I think of those men who voted for me back then . . . and recall their moral earnestness and Christian maturity, the call they extended to me ranks high above all the interview and selection proceedings that I went through later with the Prussian culture ministry or before the Berlin and Tübingen faculties. In the vote of those men [in Bern] the church was truly at work."

All his life Schlatter understood his academic office as a position dedicated not only to scientific goals but also, and most of all, to the church of Jesus Christ.

4

Beginning
of Academic
Teaching Career
in Bern

In early May 1880 Schlatter and his wife moved to
Bern. He did not know that the months to come would go
down as the most difficult of his life. Standing between Schlatter and completion of his doctoral dissertation (*Habilitation*)
would be a mountain range of unforeseeable obstacles. The
young pastor was about to be sorely tried.

The difficulties began directly upon arrival in Bern. In order
to get his work underway as quickly as possible, Schlatter
paid a courtesy call to Friedrich Nippold, professor of church
history, who at that time was the most influential man on
the faculty. Schlatter received the most discouraging reception imaginable. When he broached the topic of his doctoral
aspirations, Nippold replied, "The only thing you need to do
is pack your suitcase immediately and go back where you
came from." Obviously Nippold, who "was passionately bat-
tling the Pietists in Bern," feared that Schlatter's addition to

16. Bern, Switzerland, in the 1880s

the faculty would give too much influence to positive-biblical theology. Yet he could not actually prevent Schlatter from at least attempting to achieve professorial status. For better or for worse he had to accept Schlatter's request to sit the examinations necessary for attaining his goal.

Schlatter was naturally shaken by the hostile reception from Nippold. But he was not easily deterred. He took up work on his dissertation dealing with John the Baptist. This treatise was, along with additional testing, requisite for receiving the "Venia legendi," official permission to teach.

The coming weeks were extraordinarily difficult for Schlatter. Every morning he had to teach at the Lerber Gymnasium. In the afternoon he taught at the teachers' college. At the same time, and under great time pressure, he wrote his dissertation in order to be able to begin offering lectures at the university during the coming winter semester. In addition, his father was terminally ill, and plans had to be made to deal with the development. In spite of such unsatisfactory conditions Schlatter was able to complete his almost two hundred-page dissertation after only a few weeks of strenuous effort. He submitted it to the faculty on July 1, 1880.

Later Schlatter reminisced about the pressure he felt from the combined weight of his father's failing health and the demands of his dissertation: "On the last night I wrote non-stop, never going to bed, until five in the morning. I handed my work to my wife and told her, 'There, take it to the dean.' Then I frantically caught a train to my father's bedside where I found him barely conscious. I heard the last words he spoke as the strength to talk ebbed away."

Schlatter was deeply moved by his final encounter with his father: "As I reminded him of the glorious grace of Jesus, he replied to me, 'May the Lord preserve you in this testimony.' That was the last thing my father said to me. His thoughts were not for himself but for me. His request became a force in my life, holding me near to Jesus with intensity." Stephan Schlatter died a few days later, on July 5, 1880. His exemplary faith marked Schlatter throughout life and shaped his spiritual existence even though he felt it necessary to strike out in another theological direction in some respects.

After submitting his dissertation and weathering his father's death Schlatter had to wait to be granted the privilege of taking an imposing battery of exams. This waiting period became a grueling test of his patience, indeed of his nerves, since the faculty members chose this moment to take up the time-consuming task of establishing a protocol for attaining professorial status. Since the faculty was anything but thrilled with Schlatter's application, the exam procedure they decided on was intentionally quite strict: in addition to oral examinations in five subjects, Schlatter would have to write eight assigned essays under supervised conditions! Only if he passed all of these "magna cum laude" (the second-best possible mark) would the faculty be willing to confer on him the right to lecture. How much these regulations were drawn up to make Schlatter's addition to the faculty difficult if not impossible is shown by the fact that they were never applied to anyone else after that! In later instances the exam was waived, until finally, some fifteen years later, the regulations were substantially relaxed.

Adolf Schlatter

17. University of Bern (1835)

During the months that Schlatter waited for permission to take his exams, his friend Oettli fell seriously ill. He asked Schlatter to take over his Old Testament lectures for winter semester 1880–81. Weary of the seemingly interminable delay, on November 8, 1880, Schlatter impatiently wrote to the appropriate person in the culture ministry, education director Albert Bitzius (son of the well-known poet who wrote under the name Jeremias Gotthelf). Schlatter sought at least provisional permission to teach so that he could fill in for his sick friend. After writing Schlatter then decided that a visit to Bitzius would lend emphasis to his plea. But neither letter nor visit was effective. In fact, his importunity caused an adverse reaction among the Bern professors, who unbeknownst to Schlatter had finally decided on a *Habilitation* protocol at the beginning of November. This provided an orderly route for Schlatter to obtain the permission to teach that he sought.

18. Samuel Oettli (1846–1911)

Beginning of Academic Teaching Career in Bern

The manifold difficulties that Schlatter faced in entering a teaching track are shown particularly by his visit with Bitzius in the culture ministry. He left no doubt in Schlatter's mind that he was unwilling for Schlatter to become a professor: "He said to me, 'I have nothing against you becoming an instructor on the faculty, but I assure you that I will not make you a professor. And I will also tell you why. If I make you a professor, the Pietists in this land would call it an answer to their prayers. And I refuse to give them this pleasure.'"

This remark shows with disarming openness the extent to which Schlatter's path to becoming a theological professor was by no means merely a question of scientific qualifications. In fact, it was overwhelmingly a matter of power politics in both civil and church spheres. As it turned out, Bitzius died in 1882 and was therefore unable to prevent Schlatter from being named full professor in 1888—and this at the urging of the very Bern faculty that eight years earlier had done so much to bar his path to academic teaching!

After the many difficulties recounted above, Schlatter was able to sit his exams in December 1880. In spite of his "sparse preparation" he passed "in praiseworthy fashion" according to faculty resolution. His overall mark of "magna cum laude" was never bested in subsequent decades. Even Nippold conceded respect for Schlatter's "knowledge" and "giftedness," giving Schlatter's essays on church history and history of dogma the highest possible grade of "summa cum laude." And

19. Schlatter in Bern, 1880

Nippold did this although, he said, "Herr Licentiate Schlatter's point of view is practically the opposite of the results of my own historical investigations in all significant critical questions."

There can be no doubt that the faculty took pains to provide a just assessment of Schlatter's examination performance. Still, they made Schlatter keenly aware of their distance from and hostility toward his views even after the exams: "When I stood before the faculty to offer them my sincere thanks and made the request that they please support me in my research, I had not yet completed my remarks when I was interrupted by the dean's icy voice crying, 'That's enough!'" Except for Oettli, his faculty colleagues denied Schlatter the scientific exchange that he hoped for. They placed him in an isolated position that he did not desire: "From the beginning of my work I was . . . dependent solely on myself." The start of Schlatter's professorial activities were further clouded at the end of January 1881 by a polemical column in the *Berner Post* newspaper in the January 17–22 issue. In an article entitled "Who actually calls professors to the Bern Protestant theological faculty, anyway?" Nippold polemicized heatedly against the initiatives taken by Bern Pietists in the matter of faculty selection.

Despite all impediments Schlatter was finally able to begin lecturing in January 1881—in the middle of a semester that was already underway. The course title was "Old Testament Theology," the topic that his friend Oettli had announced but could not carry out due to serious illness.

In the coming years Schlatter's goal was twofold. On the one hand, he did not wish to disappoint the hopes for a biblically grounded theology that he shared with the Bern Pietists. On the other hand, he wanted to dispel the fears of his faculty colleagues through solid scientific writings. Trust in the Bible *and* scientific investigation of Scripture, faith *and* understanding, confessing *and* researching were to be united in his academic work. He had learned from J. T. Beck that through comprehensive contemplation of Holy Scripture false theological alternatives could be overcome. Now Schlatter saw the opportunity to overcome the false alternatives of the liberal scientific focus that sacrificed the authority of Scripture, on the one hand, and a belief in the Bible that was the enemy of science, on the other. He could show that faith did not hamper or eliminate a scientific understanding of Scripture; it rather made it possible and even enhanced it.

Schlatter served on the Bern faculty for eight years. During that time he made use of all the mental energy at his disposal to carry out scientific investigation of Scripture that was as unbiased as possible and based on rigorous observation. Yet this was to be united with credible submission to the authority of Holy Scripture, a submission that characterized his theological work throughout his life. Schlatter's Bern course offerings spanned an astonishing diversity of themes—not only Old and New Testament but also church history, systematic theology, and philosophy. It hardly needs mentioning that such thematic breadth was achieved only at the price of enormous industry. During his Bern years Schlatter often toiled until late into the night.

As a result of the brilliance of his lectures in both form and content Schlatter won increasing interest and trust from his students. An example is the later religious socialist and theology professor Hermann Kutter, who felt a close affinity to him. But his colleagues, too, expressed their respect. For example, in April 1883 the faculty recognized Schlatter's visible success as a teacher by recommending unanimously to the culture minister that he receive publicly funded remuneration for his teaching services. Again at the end of 1887 they energetically supported his promotion to associate professor. In a letter to the culture ministry dated December 19, 1887 they praised not only Schlatter's scientific accomplishments but also his "great tact and laudable discretion" on the basis of which "even colleagues with opposing theological views enjoyed only positive relations with him." While

Adolf Schlatter

Schlatter never benefited from the collegial scientific exchange that he had hoped for at Bern, such testimonies show that the tense interpersonal climate that marked the start of his activity there gradually improved as a result of his academic achievements and integrity of character.

An essential factor in Schlatter's growing acceptance by his Bern colleagues was his prize-winning monograph *Der Glaube im Neuen Testament* (*Faith in the New Testament*), a scientific breakthrough that also won him international recognition. Here is how it happened. In 1882 Schlatter responded to a call for entries in a competition sponsored by the Hague Society for the Defense of Christianity. The theme was "Belief and Believing in the New Testament." Schlatter did not have much free time in the summer of that year, and as the months passed "the deadline loomed just ahead. The book had to be in Hague by December 15th; I asked the post office how long a parcel would take to get there and worked right up to the last minute. It needed to be well written to avoid being rejected. In my haste, at the last minute I knocked my ink well over on the pages of my manuscript! But in the end I managed to submit on time."

In September 1883 Schlatter learned that his entry had won the competition. Published in 1885 after some reworking of the manuscript and consisting of nearly six hundred pages, this book is doubtless the most significant treatise on the topic of "faith" since the Reformation, unequaled even today as a comprehensive presentation of the New Testament understanding of that subject. Its appeal lies partially in the masterful theological overview of the conceptions of faith implied by the various writings that make up the New Testament. But it is also impressive because of the astounding philological care with which Schlatter investigated numerous sources, both Greek and Hebrew, which were hardly heard of at that time. In this way Schlatter could present the pre-Christian understandings of faith that prevailed in Judaism in both Palestine and in more purely Hellenistic regions. Schlatter's dis-

20. Nydeggkirche in Bern (1863)

tinctive exegesis, combining theological-pneumatic and historical-philological interpretation of Scripture, found its first high-water mark in this monograph.

In contrast to Protestant theology of his time, Schlatter's work amounted to a corrective. He placed unusually strong emphasis on love in defining faith rather than exhausting faith's meaning in the categories of thought, will, and action. Yet he did not neglect the side of faith that the Reformation placed in the foreground, the side stressing faith as the means of being declared righteous and receiving assurance of redemption.

Naturally Schlatter's award-winning book had its detractors, but even the critical reviews could not destroy the decisive importance of it for Schlatter's subsequent scientific career: in the eight years after the book was published he received calls to the faculties of Halle, Kiel, Greifswald, Basle,

21. Bern cathedral

Heidelberg, Marburg, and Bonn. Besides this large monograph Schlatter published about sixty shorter essays, talks, Bible expositions, and book reviews during his Bern sojourn. A number of these were popular presentations for a wide readership. Schlatter felt a responsibility not only to the academic world, but also to the less educated circles of Christian believers.

For this reason, while in Bern Schlatter was willingly available as a conference speaker for annual Christian gatherings. He gave public lectures in the building that housed Bern's casino and preached in the Nydegg church, in the chapel of the city hospital, and in the Münster church. His sermons, which he felt "always came together for the first time in the pulpit," left a deep impression on the hearers. As one later reminisced, "The little man's word was weighty. Every listener felt something of the large spirit living in his small stature. His speech poured forth a wealth of powerful mental concentration."

A sixteen-part series on the Book of Romans delivered in the winter of 1885–86 met broad public acclaim. Schlatter held the talks in a room of the New School for Girls. The audience consisted of people of all classes. Among the regular attenders was the world-famous surgeon Kocher. In his lectures—in preparation for which Schlatter worked through the sixteen best commentaries on Romans he could find!— he is reported to have interpreted Romans "entirely free of any notes whatsoever" and "with the greatest liveliness" at a level that all could understand. After each presentation he wrote "until late in the night" to capture the substance of what he had said. This became the ground floor of his exposition of Romans that was published in 1887. This book, in turn, was the start of his ten-volume *Erläuterungen zum Neuen Testament (Commentary on the New Testament)*. Here Schlatter gave a running explanation of the entire New Testament aimed at the level of the average Bible reader.

In the Lerber School Schlatter gave talks on religion that were also of great importance for those who attended, among whom were the famous surgeon Fritz de Quervain and the renowned theologian Theodor Schrenk. After a short extemporary prayer Schlatter would read the Greek New Testament with his students. This engrossing introduction to Scripture caused one pupil with initial interests in the natural sciences to shift his academic direction over to the study of theology in a time span of about three months. Eventually he would be known as Bern pastor Robert Friedli. He wrote of Schlatter's talks, "Here for the first time in my life I found a teacher who interpreted the New Testament with inner power. From him I gained the impression that he lived entirely in it and understood its ultimate depths." In coming years many other students who studied with Schlatter would be moved in similar ways.

A milestone for Schlatter and his wife during the Bern years was the birth of their first child in 1885. After seven childless years, they were overjoyed at the arrival on June 2 of a son, named Theodor out of gratitude to God. For Schlatter it was fitting that the long-awaited child came into the world in exactly the same year that his book on faith appeared. In the next seven years four more children were born: another son, Paul (1888), and three daughters, Hedwig (1887), Dora (1890), and Ruth (1892).

Soon after his promotion on May 14, 1888, to associate professor of New Testament and systematic theology, Schlatter was approached by the famous Greek scholar and biblical theologian Hermann Cremer at the theological seminary in Greifswald. Would Schlatter be willing to serve as full professor on the faculty there? Shortly thereafter he received a telegram on a Sunday morning from Prussian culture minister Althoff, who wished to meet with Schlatter in Berlin two days hence. On the appointed day Schlatter appeared—in defiance of etiquette, without the obligatory formal attire including white gloves—and Minister Althoff formally offered him the Greifswald chair. "The official wanted to nail me down on the spot, but I said that I would have to talk with my wife first. He replied that he had known for a long time that calls to academic posts hinged on wives' decisions."

22. The Schlatter children (from left to right): Paul, Dora, Hedwig, Theodor, Ruth

Upon returning Schlatter discussed the matter with his wife, then conveyed to Althoff his willingness to accept the call to Greifswald. For Schlatter what tipped the scales was the prospect of a lecture hall "that was incomparably larger and more conducive to teaching than anything Bern could offer." But even more important was his hope for fruitful working relations with like-minded colleagues who shared his vision for a biblical renewal of Protestant theology.

The rector of the University of Bern received word of Schlatter's impending departure with surprise, since he had turned down a call from Kiel a brief time earlier. The rector, who had a good relationship with Schlatter, had already planned a celebration in honor of Schlatter's continuing presence at Bern. When he learned of the altered situation, the celebration was "still held—but as a going away party!"

Schlatter's decision to leave his Swiss homeland and assume the chair in Greifswald was of decisive importance for his wife and him alike: "The switch into service in the Prussian setting changed . . . everything that I was and did . . . profoundly." Not until they were relocated in the Pomeranian lowlands did Schlatter become fully aware of what he must leave behind: "It wasn't the magnificence of Switzerland that held me there; I said good-bye to it easily. I knew, of course, that it is a beautiful place and enjoyed its beauty richly in my youth during the innumerable days that we roamed from the mountains of Säntis to the shores of Lake Constance. Likewise there was the beauty of Kilchberg and Neumünster, where I had Lake Zurich before me every time I went to church. And then there was Bern, where I had a view of the Bern Alps from the balcony of my study; there too we savored rare but doubly enjoyable holidays when we retreated to the most glorious corners of Switzerland. . . . But shortly before my departure we gathered with dear fellow believers in a village of the Emmental region [near Bern]. Oettli said to me, 'Take one more look at the Emmental Mountains; you won't be seeing them anymore.' I was taken aback by the way he seemed to be thinking. Should I give a care about such trifles? . . . But when I stood in the flatlands of Greifswald—where there is nothing but flatlands—I sensed how profoundly we are embedded in our environment. And when I returned to Switzerland on holiday, and when the mountains of my homeland rose before me as we crossed Lake Constance, the rejoicing of my soul was proof of the oppressiveness of my homesickness. But even then my conviction was not shaken that a fruitful place of service would make every sacrifice worthwhile."

5

Joint Work with Cremer in Greifswald

Immediately after the end of the 1888 summer semester, Schlatter and his family relocated to Greifswald, where they were warmly received by Hermann Cremer. Schlatter used his summer holidays to make good on an old promise by writing *Einleitung in die Bibel* (*Introduction to the Bible*). The promise had been made to David Gundert of Calwer Publishers, who asked Schlatter to write a book on that subject aimed at a wide readership. Schlatter penned the book, which ran over five hundred pages, in such an incredibly brief time that it was available already at the beginning of 1889. His goal was to enable the reader to "break through the whole swarm of opinions" that hung over Scripture like a cloud and to furnish access to that "which the Bible itself testifies." Schlatter's *Introduction* received a lively reception from many (Cremer among them), but met opposition from certain Pietists, since in some historical questions (e.g., source theories of Old Testament books) Schlatter took positions that were felt by some to be too accommodating of contemporary biblical criticism.

Adolf Schlatter

23. Hermann Cremer (1834–1903)

In the 1888–89 winter semester Schlatter began joint labor with Hermann Cremer (1834–1903). Cremer had become famous among his academic peers most of all through his great *Biblisch-theologisches Wörterbuch* (*Biblical-Theological Dictionary*) of New Testament Greek. Cremer was eighteen years older than Schlatter and saw himself furthering the tradition established by the Württemberg Bible scholar Johann Albrecht Bengel. The fruit of their shared labor far exceeded Schlatter's expectations. The time was so productive and favorable that Schlatter would later regard the years at Greifswald as the most pleasant of his whole academic career.

24. Greifswald—town market and Church of Mary

The close cooperation that developed between the two scholars, easy to take for granted in hindsight, was by no means assured at the time. There were marked differences between the two men in their personalities (Cremer was a melancholy Westphalian, Schlatter a temperamental Swiss) and in their church preferences (Cremer was a highly loyal Lutheran, Schlatter more eclectic in his ecclesial ties). It was therefore not self-evident that they would discover a deep commonality between them. But their contrasting distinctives did not extend to the starting point and goal of their theological work. The starting point for both was most emphatically Holy Scripture. Both wanted to be consistent biblical theologians who avoided every "divergence from Scripture" and every "self-proclaimed mastery over the Scriptures by the theologian." And both set the goal of their theological research as "a theology of belief" that would lead to Jesus Christ, the crucified and resurrected Lord, and the sole ground of faith.

This goal also marked the personal relationship between the two: the secret of their extraordinary closeness was their oneness in a shared faith, their brotherly tie in Christ. This formed the basis of a spiritual fellowship that caused all theological differences to recede into the background: "Cremer too was first of all a Christian, and then as a result and secondly a churchman; he was first bound to Christ, and for that reason he was a member of the fellowship united in Christ. That is how the son of a Westphalian Pietist and the son of a Swiss Baptist could effortlessly join hands." In addition to a shared faith there arose a deep bond of love from which sprang a manly friendship of rare depth. "In collegial dealings" Cremer was "touchingly selfless and full of humility, just as he was convinced that his colleague [Schlatter] did not seek his own greatness and honor but, like Cremer, was submitted to Christ rather than bent on himself."

This mutual bond was ultimately sealed by their shared aversion to liberal theology. At the time its most influential form was the so-called Ritschlian school (named for Albrecht Ritschl, 1822–89), whose most important proponents were Wilhelm Herrmann (1846–1922) and Adolf von Harnack (1851–1930). Cremer and Schlatter both saw here a dangerous threat to the biblical gospel. Both bore a burden to formulate an academically well-grounded biblical alternative to Ritschlian thinking, which at that time was enjoying a triumphal advance through German theological faculties. The melancholy Cremer strove for a "preservation of the gospel through the present long winter's night" in the theological faculties, while the optimistic and choleric Schlatter dared to hope for the onset of a new spring. (In a letter to Cremer on December 31, 1897, Schlatter asked, "Must winter last forever?")

The felicitous tie between Schlatter and Cremer was supplemented with an unusually friendly working relationship with other faculty members: Zöckler, Schultze, von Nathusius, Baethgen, and Giesebrecht. The whole group enjoyed close relations with each other. It is no exaggeration to say that under Cremer and Schlatter the Greifswald theology fac-

25. University of Greifswald

ulty bloomed as it never had before, reaching the high point of its history. Students streamed to Greifswald in droves to hear Cremer and Schlatter. They came from all over Germany and Switzerland and even from Finland, England, and America! Greifswald became an internationally known center of positive-biblical theology. In coming to Greifswald Schlatter hoped to find a site for his work that would be more satisfactory than the situation in Bern. This hope was fulfilled to an extent that he could not have dreamed.

Schlatter's teaching at Greifswald covered primarily New Testament exegesis and research into Judaism. But systematic theology was an area of interest as well. In the summer semester of 1892 he lectured for the first time on Christian dogmatics. In Greifswald Schlatter found one of his most gifted students, the later New Testament theologian and systematician Wilhelm Lütgert (1863–1938). With Schlatter's encouragement Lütgert produced the pathbreaking study *Die Liebe im Neuen Testament* (*Love in the New Testament*) that complemented his teacher's *Der Glaube im Neuen Testament* (*Faith in the New Testament*). Lütgert's four-volume *Geschichte des Idealismus* (*History of Idealism*) and systematic works like *Schöpfung und Offenbarung* (*Creation and Revelation*) and *Ethik der Liebe* (*Ethics of Love*) took up

26. Schlatter in 1890

many Schlatterian impulses and furthered them in independent ways.

A memorable episode from the Greifswald years was a trip to Palestine granted and financed by the ministry of culture. Together with four others from Switzerland (among them Samuel Oettli) Schlatter toured Italy, Egypt, Palestine, and Greece. "The weeks were chock full, with hardly a day passing without indelible, colorful images being planted in my soul." The trip focused on Palestine, which the five men crisscrossed with horses and tents. Schlatter's thirst for archaeological and topographical knowledge was wonderfully satisfied by the expedition. After his return he summarized the scientific harvest of his observations in a book entitled *Zur Topographie und Geschichte Palästinas* (*The Topography and History of Palestine*)—a work that was ruthlessly criticized by the liberal church historian Emil Schürer.

In summary, Schlatter's time at Greifswald was important in terms of unique teaching conditions and opportunities to exert theological influence on the next generation. Another high point was the camaraderie with Hermann Cremer. The Greifswald years gave birth to a lifelong friendship and professional association between them that bore extensive fruit: an intensive exchange of letters; a technical biblical and theological journal (*Beiträge zur Förderung christlicher Theologie*, founded in 1897); repeated common appearances at theological conferences (e.g., the "Theologische Wochen" at Bethel). And Cremer's theological influence on Schlatter is not to be minimized, for in Cremer Schlatter encountered a combination of Lutheran churchmanship and biblical piety that left an enduring impression: "For Cremer the grace of Jesus consisted in the forgiveness of sins. . . . To listen to him tirelessly praise this gift of divine grace produced delight, assistance, purification, and strength. In this way he did not only clarify for me devoted Lutheranism; he also led me with penetrating force to Scripture—and not just to Paul, but most of all to Jesus, to whose cross Cremer directed our gaze in such a way as to cause faith to desire the fruit of his cross." If the Lutheran theologian Paul Althaus is correct that on the whole Schlatter's theology inclines more to the Lutheran than to the Reformed tradition, this finding is to a considerable degree the result of Schlatter's encounter with Hermann Cremer.

It was for Schlatter one of life's more painful turns that the happy Greifswald days came to an end after only five years. Theologically concerned circles in the German Protestant church had demanded of the kaiser that he establish a professorship at Berlin University that would uphold orthodoxy against the liberalism of Adolf von Harnack and his

Adolf Schlatter

27. Adolf and Susanna Schlatter with children Paul (left), Hedwig, and Theodor (1889)

colleagues. This move was spawned by Harnack's critical posture over against the Apostles' Creed. The ministry of culture was prepared to fulfill this demand in spite of the determined opposition of the university faculty. After the ministry of culture first tried to hire Martin Kähler, well-known biblical theologian in Halle, and then Hermann Cremer, Schlatter was approached in January 1893 to accept the new chair. Schlatter was no more inclined to answer this call than were Kähler and Cremer. But in March 1893 culture minister Althoff made one more intensive effort to woo Schlatter to Berlin. Schlatter insistently declined, until Althoff excitedly divulged that he would lose his job if Schlatter refused. At this point, in spite of misgivings, Schlat-

28. The official pronouncement of Schlatter's appointment at Greifswald issued by Kaiser Wilhelm I

ter gave in. It was not until later that he realized what painful consequences this decision would have, not only for him but for his friend Cremer. For both of them their working relationship possessed a unique character.

Schlatter speaks of how deeply shaken he was at the thought of separation from his old friend: "Now when I had to tell Cremer how the battle with Althoff ended, I totally lost my train of thought in my anxiety over the task that awaited me in Berlin. At this point Cremer selflessly and bravely encouraged me, and I heard not even one hard or biting word from him, although I knew that I had wounded him by giving in to Althoff." It is understandable that both men found it extraordinarily difficult to give up their fruitful joint work after only five years. And it is likewise not hard to see why the time leading up to the move to Berlin was somewhat depressing for Schlatter.

In the "dark weeks that followed the decision" in favor of Berlin Schlatter was, however, comforted by the words of 1 John 4:4, which the apostle John had used to strengthen the faithful in their conflict with false teaching: "Greater is he that is in you than he that is in the world." Schlatter accepted this verse as helpful guidance for his relocation to the Prussian capital, where the important liberal theologian Adolf von Harnack was on the verge of leading the theological faculty into international prominence. But being left behind hit Hermann Cremer hard. He wrote to Schlatter (July 17, 1898), "Why do we have to part? Yes, why? Should I regard it as punishment for something I've done? I am often burdened by this thought. I pray all the more urgently that the Lord my God might not reject my toil in his service and that he would help me to work more selflessly than before."

6

Professor of Systematics in Berlin

In numerous respects the change from the quiet provincial town of Greifswald to the world-class city of Berlin was a big adjustment for Schlatter. His sense of closeness to nature prohibited him from feeling at home in a city of over a million people, especially given his sharp eye for the daunting social and moral ills that marked Berlin. Add to this the completely new situation of the faculty: in view of the strong liberal leanings of Schlatter's colleagues, profound commonalities of viewpoint on matters of substance were hardly to be expected. The fact that he was awarded the chair against faculty wishes by decision of state authorities did not make the conditions of his starting months at Berlin easy. The result for Schlatter was a climate of cordiality but aloofness between him and his colleagues.

And yet there was a noteworthy exception from a quarter that Schlatter did not expect: the one man on the faculty who was most nearly Schlatter's theological opposite, the famous Adolf von Harnack (1851–1930), received him from the very start with unusual friendliness and openness! Schlatter's deci-

29. Kant Street in Berlin, where the Schlatter family lived

sion to come to Berlin had hardly been announced when Harnack wrote him—although he was against the way that the chair Schlatter occupied had been decreed from above: "Now I am happy that you are coming, and these lines are meant to let you know that" (March 9, 1893). And the first discussion between them had a thoroughly positive tone: "I had ... a very nice exchange with Harnack, open and penetrating. We talked about nearly everything of note in the present world of scientific interchange" (letter to Cremer, November 8, 1893).

In the months to come an ongoing and substantial discussion developed between the two theologians, each so different in his views, covering a full range of theological topics. This discussion was both oral and written. What Schlatter sought in vain in Bern now became a reality in Berlin: amicable scientific exchange that could transcend even deeply felt theological differences. This did not mean that the differences were suppressed. Once, in the company of other faculty members, Harnack stated, "All that separates me from my colleague Schlatter is the question of miracles." Schlatter shot back spiritedly, "No, the question of God!" Later,

30. Adolf von Harnack (1851–1930)

when Schlatter moved from Berlin to Tübingen, Harnack sincerely felt the loss and expressly missed the animated intellectual exchange: "I miss our discussions and feel it as a serious loss that I have no one around me who can by challenging my views make me ponder them" (letter of February 5, 1899).

As professor of systematic theology Schlatter was obligated most of all to lecture in the area of dogmatics. But he reserved the right to lecture on New Testament themes, too. While at Berlin he taught Christian ethics for the first time in his life.

Adolf Schlatter

In these lectures he apparently succeeded in reaching precisely those students most disturbed by the secular slant of contemporary philosophy. The later Bethel professor Theodor Oestreicher made this observation: "Along with the New Testament we read . . . Kant, Schopenhauer, Nietzsche, and the latest literature . . . often enough our faith was like a city under siege by the enemy Skepticism." From "our theological professors . . . [we] found . . . no help whatsoever. They confined themselves to the domain of their theological subject matter. How we pricked up our ears when Schlatter came along and began to deal exhaustively with Kant's ethical foundation in the context of his overall outlook; when he examined the tenability of Schopenhauer's morality of compassion; when he settled accounts with Nietzsche's *Beyond Good and Evil*! Suddenly light swept across the whole range of modern thought! We were astonished at the thoroughness and fearlessness with which Schlatter proceeded."

But the students were fascinated not only by the way Schlatter pointed out the errors of modern thought. They were also struck by how he unfolded the alternative of "a positive Christian doctrine of life possessing undreamed-of depth and breadth on the basis of biblical statements." Schlatter's student Oestreicher continues, "The result for us was the confidence that we could uphold our Christian outlook with good conscience and joy even in the corrosive atmosphere of current thought."

The decade of the 1890s saw Schlatter venture to offer comprehensive overviews of large, overarching bodies of material in the areas of systematic and New Testament theology. If in Greifswald he had offered lectures on "Christian Dogmatics" for the first time (1892–93), now in Berlin he added "Christian Ethics" (1894) and, in exegesis, "History of Jesus" (1894) and "New Testament Theology" (1895–96). Through his specially requested exegetical lectures Schlatter was able to supplement in essential respects his courses on dogmatic and ethical subjects. If in systematics lectures he could devote

31. Schlatter in 1895

himself entirely to the problems of modern thought, in his New Testament lectures he had an opportunity to introduce his students to the Word of God at the basic level and in that way acquaint them with the foundations of the faith.

It was Schlatter's concern to carry out faith-supporting exegesis that understood Scripture as its basis, starting point, and norm. Such an exegesis must stand without reserve in the service of Scripture. It must take seriously not only the human but also the divine side of the Bible. It must give voice to the contents of the Bible without abbreviation or manipulation. Accordingly Schlatter impressed on his Berlin students what exegesis, rightly understood, means: "Seeing what is there before your eyes!" And it was a great event for listening students to observe Schlatter's exegetical reasoning unfold as it attempted to do justice to the human-divine double character of Scripture. This exegesis was both historical and pneumatic, philological and theological: "With Schlatter exegesis was no longer boring historical-critical science but real theology, a serious harking to God and his Word. We learned actually to see what lay before our eyes, and what we saw was so unsettlingly serious and vast that one lost all appetite for historical-critical trifling with this Word."

At Berlin Schlatter took steps to initiate contact with students outside the university setting, too. He held regular Bible studies at the Berlin Young Men's Christian Association (YMCA), headed up by Herr von Rothkirch. He also made himself available to the German Christian Student Consortium (GCSC) under Graf Pückler. While he labored fruitfully in the YMCA setting, relations were less relaxed with the GCSC because Schlatter viewed Graf Pückler's Neo-Pietistic understanding of conversion as an unbiblical oversimplification.

Schlatter also struck up worthwhile contact with the famous Protestant theologian and social reformer Adolf Stoecker (1835–1909), whom he met at the home of the Reformed preacher Dalton. Stoecker worked toward not only thoroughgoing social reform on a monarchical basis but also better representation of positive-biblical theology in the theological faculties. Schlatter supported Stoecker's initiative and accordingly in 1895 took part in a Protestant convention called by Stoecker. This gathering produced a declaration (authored by Schlatter) decrying the overwhelming dominance of theological liberalism on theological faculties. To Schlatter's surprise a storm of protest arose among his Berlin colleagues, who felt that the declaration was damaging to the status and high honor of the professorial office. Even after a lively faculty meeting, however, Schlatter could not bring himself to regret his involvement in the convention: "For me the choice stands sharply defined: God's believing community or professional colleagues? And my decision was as clear as the choice . . . faith is more than knowledge, and church more than faculty" (letter to Cremer, May 21, 1895).

Schlatter's second Berlin acquaintance of far-reaching importance grew out of his contact with the man known by some as the "apostle of love," Friedrich von Bodelschwingh (1831–1910), founder of a well-known epileptic clinic.[1] Schlatter met Bodelschwingh at meetings of the East Africa Mission in Berlin. In view of the increasing tension between scientific theology and the church, Bodelschwingh was already pursuing a plan to start a private theological school at Bethel with the Bible as its basis. He courted Schlatter's involvement and support during his Berlin years. At first, Schlatter reacted negatively to the idea. He was more interested in strengthening biblically oriented theology in existing theological faculties. But Bodelschwingh could not be dissuaded, and after some years finally won Schlatter over to his side.

The two men had an intensive encounter lasting several days in the summer of 1897. Schlatter had finished speaking at a conference in Werningerode (Harz) in north-central Germany and traveled to nearby Braunlage. Bodelschwingh happened to be on vacation there and invited Schlatter to spend a few days with him. The professor, ready for a break, gladly accepted the invitation. Bodelschwingh's vigor, energy, and courageous love—he was already sixty-six years old at the time—made such a deep impression on Schlatter that he privately wondered whether he should have stayed in the pastorate after all. For there were "tasks of gigantic proportions that confront us as our nation plunges ever deeper into sickness and godlessness," and in such a climate scientific work could seem to amount to "frivolous child's play."

Yet as the friendship and working relationship between them developed, it became clear that their respective distinctive contributions—Schlatter's teaching and Bodel-

---

1. [Located near Bielefeld, between Münster and Hannover in northwestern Germany, Bethel was founded in 1867 by Bodelschwingh to care for epileptics and others as a convalescent home and asylum. By the early 1930s it cared for some 2500 epileptics and 800 with other disorders. Patients who were able worked at farm and other productive communal activities under the supervision of both male and female personnel from the German Protestant church diaconate. The unemployed and homeless were likewise assured work and medical attention. Over the years four sister institutions spun off the Bethel model. In addition to local social relief work there was an extensive educational program for theological, missionary, and nurses training (source: 1932 edition of Der Große Herder, vol. 2, pp. 551f.).]

32. Humboldt University of Berlin, 1900 (founded in 1809 as Friedrich Wilhelm University)

schwingh's merciful love—supplemented each other. Schlatter proposed that in the future a week-long theological conference be held at Bethel to give an opportunity for biblically oriented university professors to engage in theological labor with a large body of pastors. This would underscore and strengthen the inseparable bond between theology and church. That the location of these conferences was Bethel, not some academic venue, was a fitting tribute to the inner solidarity of truth and love, knowledge and action. Bodelschwingh agreed to Schlatter's proposal "without hesitation," and the very next year the first "Theological Week" took place, with Hermann Cremer among those playing a leading role.

Another Berlin development for Schlatter was the founding of a new theological journal, already mentioned earlier, which Schlatter and Cremer co-edited. It was called *Beiträge zur Förderung christlicher Theologie* (*Essays for the Furtherance of Christian Theology*). Younger friends of Schlatter and Cremer, Wilhelm Lütgert and Erich Schraeder, had urged them to found it. Lütgert and Schraeder, proponents of the "Greifswald School," saw the need for a publication that would carry positive-biblically oriented scientific essays and treatises. Schlatter made his decision to support this initiative while on a solitary mountain hike near Eisenach in central Germany. Schlatter recalls the setting was one of "pouring rain . . . and refreshing stillness." The journal would publicize the labor of positive-biblically oriented theologians for some five decades after its beginning in 1897.

The first issue of this journal carried perhaps the most important publication that Schlatter wrote during his Berlin years: "Der Dienst des Christen in der älteren Dogmatik" ("The Ministry of the Christian in Older Dogmatics"). In this groundbreaking study Schlatter showed the neglect of love and works in the theology of Lutheran and Reformed orthodoxy in the post-Reformation generations. Schlatter grew increasingly certain that this shortcoming was grounded in an abbreviation and neglect of the doctrine of love by the Reformers themselves.

Schlatter's goal in this essay was to show that the New Testament challenged adherents of *all* current theological positions—including the biblical-positive!—to free themselves from restrictive traditions that stood in the way of the full expression of divine truth and love. This essay was of programmatic importance for the new journal, serving notice that mere rehearsal of

33. Theodor von Häring (1848–1928), systematics professor at Tübingen

conservative views would not suffice; only a more profound appropriation of the New Testament would do.

In the autumn of 1897 Schlatter was asked whether he would consider moving to Tübingen in southwestern Germany to assume a theological chair at the university there. The "Protestant-Church Coalition," a group representing the interests of Pietism in the Württemberg region, had passed a resolution requesting the government to establish a new teaching chair. The person who occupied it would support "biblical truth and church confession." The Tübingen systematician Theodor Häring (1848–1928), who had been on good terms with Schlatter for some years, had already inquired in strict confidence on February 15, 1897, whether Schlatter would be interested in such a position. It would be an appointment primarily in the area of New Testament, which (if Schlatter came) in Württemberg would mean a "continuation of the work of Bengel and Beck under altered historical conditions."[2] After Schlatter received a positive answer to his question whether he would be allowed to give lectures in systematics, too, he finally agreed to the move on November 4, 1897.

It was not an easy decision. Culture minister Althoff did everything in his power to keep Schlatter in Berlin. Decisive for Schlatter was the conviction that Tübingen was "more conducive" to his "central theological task, interpretation of Scripture, doctrinal formation, etc." In addition there was the desire for a final site of activity to end Schlatter's moves from academic place to place. No university town in Germany was so well suited to measure up to Schlatter's goals as Tübingen: "From my student days there, Tübingen retained a bright glow for me. I was glad to be Beck's successor. . . . I expected that Tübingen would end my years of moving about; it would be a real home. There I could again see the sun in the heav-

---

2. [Johann Albrecht Bengel (1687–1752) was a famous Schwabian New Testament scholar and churchman who trained at Tübingen. J. T. Beck (1804–78; see ch. 2 above) in many ways furthered Bengel's heritage. For a sympathetic assessment of both men, see Gerhard Maier, Biblical Hermeneutics, trans. by R. Yarbrough (Wheaton: Crossway, 1994).]

34. Adolf and Susanna Schlatter with their children: Dora, Theodor, Ruth, Hedwig, Paul

ens and the hills, fields, and forests of the earth. And I would have a lecture setting that would facilitate fruitful interchange with those engaged in study."

In the call to Tübingen Schlatter saw the welcome opportunity to get away from the "inner calm" of the world-class city of Berlin, which he felt to be enervating. Tübingen would be a place combining intellectual growth with the prospects of productive and far-reaching theological activity. And so it happened that with a joyful heart Schlatter left Berlin in early January 1898 and headed for Tübingen, where he hoped for "a new version of Greifswald" (letter to Cremer, November 4, 1897). The Berlin years marked the end of his academic apprenticeship, so to speak; in Tübingen he found "his niche"—the location that would see him rise to the high point of his effectiveness.

7

High Point of Schlatter's Effectiveness in Tübingen

Schlatter began teaching at the University of Tübingen in the summer semester of 1898. After the Berlin appointment in systematic theology he now—as in Bern and Greifswald—held a chair of New Testament. He could again devote himself entirely to the area that stood at the center of his theological researches. But Schlatter had no intention of becoming hyperspecialized. He therefore received assurances from the appropriate Württemberg authorities that he had the right to offer lectures in dogmatics. Thus in Tübingen it was not only his exegetical but also his systematic teaching activity that reached its high point, although after 1914 his systematics lectures and studies finally receded into the background.

The start of Schlatter's work in Tübingen was not without difficulties. Many of the students regarded the newcomer as a pious but unscientific biblicist. Considerable interest surrounded the occasion of his inaugural lecture, "The New

35. Schlatter lecturing

Testament and the Contemporary Theology of Jerusalem,"
held in the facilities of the Tübingen theology faculty. Fritz
von Bodelschwingh Jr. witnessed the event and left behind
the following impression: "Every seat in the large lecture hall
was filled. Around us we could see that many listeners were
critical of Schlatter's views. Most Schwabians at that time
regarded Schlatter as unscientific. . . . So the room was full
of tension. Then we heard a loud crash behind us. Schlatter
had entered the room and forcefully flung the door closed
behind him. The old building seemed to be shaken to its foundations. As the new professor stepped quickly to the podium
and began his lecture without a word of introduction, some
of us had the feeling that in this moment the door of a past

era of theological science had been closed. A new way into the holy land of God-taught erudition was flung open."

In fact, Schlatter's inaugural lecture—still untranslated—was a noteworthy declaration of principle. In memorable fashion Schlatter explicated the theme that was a special area of interest throughout the whole span of his New Testament research: the relationship of the New Testament to Judaism of that time. But he went a giant step further. He spoke of the great responsibility that lay on scientific theology generally, a responsibility requiring sober reflection on such an occasion in view of theology's considerable influence on the populace "for good and for ill." This responsibility could be carried out only when theology took it as a matter of first priority "that it be Christian."

36. At work, December 29, 1910

Adolf Schlatter

From the very first semester Schlatter could not complain about the attendance at his lectures. The first course he offered drew eighty to one hundred students. And yet there was an unmistakable reserve on the part of the Württemberg theology students toward Schlatter in the first years of his Tübingen labors: in his first dogmatics lectures there was only one Schwabian! The north German students streamed all the more gladly into his lecture hall!

Schlatter's move to Tübingen caused a perceptible rise in the number of theology students there. By his second semester, the number of theology students from northern Germany had tripled! Through the quality of his lectures, however, Schlatter also gradually won the respect of the Schwabian theology majors, as one of them reported in 1910 to professor of practical theology Paul Wurster: "The negative view, in principle, of Professor Schlatter held by the theology students has been left behind. He came to Tübingen marked with

37. With Paul Wurster

38. Church historian Karl Holl (1866–1926)

the label 'orthodox.' But when you get to know him you realize that this description is absolutely unfounded. He is by no means a party man and he holds himself completely aloof from all dogmatic slogans. He is a man marked most of all by deep reverence for Holy Scripture, and that can only command respect."

A factor that should not be underestimated in Schlatter's growing acceptance was presumably his famous course of lectures "Philosophy since Descartes. Its Religious and Ethical Results," which Schlatter offered in 1905–6 and again in 1908. In these lectures, attended and greatly admired by the famous church historian Karl Holl (1866–1926), Schlatter developed a remarkable analysis of the history of philosophy from Descartes to Nietzsche. His presentation received wide notice among theologians and would later be described by Helmut Thielicke as "brilliant." To Karl Holl's great regret Schlatter published his lectures in 1906 only in considerably abbreviated form.

In this course Schlatter offered valuable aid to theology majors, who had to complete a regimen of philosophical study in their first four semesters. They were given tools both to understand and to evaluate, from the standpoint of a faith taking its cue from Holy Scripture, the diverse range of questions of contemporary philosophy. It was no small challenge to the students that Schlatter often subjected contemporary philosophers to unusually sharp criticism and even condemned philosophical outlooks that were widely accepted within Protestant theology as fateful intellectual missteps. (An example here would be Kant's philosophy.) At the same time, and no less challenging for students, Schlatter attempted to avoid simplistic evaluations and to bring out the strengths and positive sides of each philosophical synthesis he treated.

In spite of the skepticism he faced from some of his hearers, Schlatter regarded his Tübingen activities as yielding "a highly rewarding professorial opportunity" from the very first semester (letter to Cremer of May 16, 1898). One deficiency that he did sense: apart from his good relations with Professor Häring, he had little contact with faculty colleagues at first. On the other hand, he enjoyed the "glorious peace" and "almost paradisical quiet" that this relative isolation brought with it. Here was a sharp contrast to the fast pace life of his Berlin years.

The unexpected death of his fifty-one-year-old wife on July 9, 1907 following an operation marked a turning point in Schlatter's life. She left her husband with five children ranging in age from fifteen to twenty-two years. The loss hit Schlatter hard, but he bore the load with valiant faith. Deeply moved he testified of his spouse, "It was her joy to have as

39. Susanna Schlatter, née Schoop

40. With daughters Hedwig (left) and Dora at Rigi-Rotstook, August 29, 1928

full a part in my work as she could, and she devoted constant care to her children. She did what she could. We commend her into God's hands." Schlatter's oldest son, Theodor, reports that Schlatter concluded the prayer at the graveside with the confession of the church father Chrysostom, "The Lord be praised for everything!"

Schlatter never remarried. He would bear the loneliness of being a widower for the next thirty-one years. But his isolation was lessened considerably by his two daughters, Hedwig (1887–1946) and Dora (1890–1969), who remained unmarried. Until his death they cared for him with great appreciation for his responsibilities as theological teacher. In those same years he found in his son, Theodor (1885–1971), an increasingly capable discussion partner regarding the pressing theological and church-state questions of the day. In 1914 Theodor Schlatter became pastor of the Tübingen theological faculty church, in 1923 professor at the theological school in Bethel, in 1934 dean at Esslingen, and finally in 1937 prelate in Ludwigsburg. The closeness of the theological and personal exchange between father and son is shown in the fact that Schlatter's archives contain some 800 letters that passed between them. In the year 1933 alone these letters fill about 350 pages; alto-

41. With son Theodor on Marmora, 1911

gether they amount to thousands of pages. Schlatter also cultivated warm ties with his daughter, Ruth (1892–1962), and (after 1916) her husband, the Württemberg pastor Friedrich Hinderer (d. 1968).

The most bitter blow that Schlatter endured following his wife's death was the severing of the deep relationship with his son, Paul. A promising academic historian, he lost his life in 1914 on the battlefield of the First World War. But the camaraderie of his other children afforded Schlatter a reservoir of joy and thankfulness, since they all lived in dedica-

42. With children outside Schlatter's Tübingen residence about 1917 (left to right): Hedwig, Ruth, Theodor, Dora

43. With son Paul, Christmas 1911

tion to the faith and sought to serve the church as pastor (Theodor), pastor's wife (Ruth), and leaders of young women's groups (Hedwig and Dora).

The harsh incursion of his wife's death gave Schlatter a sense of the relevance of eternity that he had not previously possessed: "There echoed through my soul the words, 'Get yourself ready, too.'" He saw himself compelled to finish out the life work he had begun in the light of the age to come, for in addition to the wake-up call of his wife's death he could sense his own vigor perceptibly waning. On June 21, 1908, he wrote to the professor who had succeeded him in Basle, Fritz Barth (father of Karl Barth), "I have come under the weighty impression that for me it is time to wrap up what I've begun. My strength for work is dropping off sharply."

So Schlatter applied himself to the task of consolidating his previous New Testament and systematic theological studies into three large volumes: "The first and to me dearest task was passing along the word of Jesus. I rejected the move of slotting Jesus' word into just one chapter of New Testament theology, because this would obscure the fundamental significance that it has for the church." In order to demonstrate the foundational importance of Jesus' proclamation for Christian theology, Schlatter devoted a volume of nearly six hundred pages to that proclamation. Some would call it one of the grandest presentations of the teaching and activity of Jesus that the twentieth century has produced. In masterful fashion Schlatter aptly depicted the unity of the Jesus of history and the Christ of faith. His extraordinary capacity for theological synthesis received acclaim even from critics of his work.

The concentrated labor on this comprehensive book during the summer of 1908 prevented Schlatter from accepting the repeated heartfelt invitation of the elderly Bodelschwingh to spend summer holidays with him at Bethel. Bodelschwingh, who sensed that he did not have long to live, feared he would "perhaps on this side of the grave not [be able] to see" Schlatter again (letter of August 5, 1908). Nevertheless, with a heavy heart Schlatter refused. He dared not interrupt the work on his Jesus book. Fully aware of the weight of his decision he wrote to his friend, "My decision to keep working without interruption weighs heavily on me, especially in that now I will not see you. Whether it will come about at a later time lies in the Father's hands. Permit me, however, to thank you warmly once again for the brotherly love with which you have so often refreshed, strengthened, and uplifted me" (September 19, 1908).

When Schlatter penned these lines he was unaware that it would be his farewell letter to Bodelschwingh. He would not see his friend again in this life. When Bodelschwingh passed away in 1910, a thirteen-year friendship came to an end. Schlatter counted it among the dearest relationships of his life. He had treasured the deceased's unique and wide-ranging ministries of charity, pursued with the goal of both church renewal and social transformation. For his part, Bodelschwingh saw in Schlatter a theological professor with rare gifts on two counts. First, Schlatter faithfully embodied Bodelschwingh's ideal of combining faith and science, confession and research. Second, Schlatter was committed to a renewal of theology in a scriptural sense. The joint work of these two fundamentally different yet spiritually like-minded men may certainly be reckoned among the most felicitous aspects of Schlatter's life.

After completing his book *Das Wort Jesu* (*The Word of Jesus*)—reissued in revised form in 1922 under the title *Die Geschichte des Christus* (*The History of the Christ*)—Schlatter got to work on the second volume of his New Testament theology. This appeared in 1910 as *Die Lehre der Apostel* (*The Teaching of the Apostles*). Like volume one, it filled nearly six hundred pages. In it Schlatter attempted to work out the respective distinctives of the various New Testament authors, while at the same time demonstrating the commonality in the basic doctrines of the faith that bind all the New Testament writings together.

This second volume highlighted Schlatter's understanding of both the multiformity of the one faith in Jesus and the unity that pervades and delimits a New Testament theology's diversity. He successfully overcame the dichotomy between a liberal exegesis, which disputes the unity of the New Testament canon, and an ahistorical biblicism, which does not do justice to the individual and historical peculiarities of each particular New Testament writing: "I saw . . . no rift between the work of Jesus and that of his messengers . . . , between the work of Peter in Jerusalem and that of Paul among the Greeks, but possessed a unified New Testament. . . . Therefore, alongside other depictions of the New Testament church that posited thousands of contradictions, I placed my own."

The great biblical theologian Martin Kähler (1835–1912) was—despite a few reservations—"deeply gripped" and "full of admiration" for Schlatter's both theologically and historically well-grounded "theology of the New Testament." In it he saw an "inductive proof . . . for the harmonious reality of the picture that the New Testament paints. I had always had the same impression myself but did not find the means to demonstrate it to others" (letter to Schlatter, January 3, 1910). The Kiel systematician Erich Schraeder (1861–1936) wrote to Schlatter excitedly: "Your New Testament theology is theology; I have seldom seen God so majestically and brightly in a treatment of the Bible" (letter of April 7, 1910). Even the Marburg New Testament scholar Rudolf Bultmann (1884–1976), whose views were quite different from Schlatter's, saw the "strength" of Schlatter's work "in its grasp of the New Testament's religious content."

After completing his New Testament theology Schlatter turned to his volume on dogmatics. In it he undertook the daring task of developing a transconfessional "theology of facts." Its affirmations would be grounded in both the reality of creation (nature, humanness, history) and the (histori-

44. Martin Kähler (1835–1912), theologian and New Testament exegete

cal and spiritual) realities of the revelation of Christ. And Schlatter would attempt to present this in such a way that nonbelievers, too, could basically reconstruct the affirmations. Schlatter wanted to establish that the contents of Christian theology—like the contents of other sciences—rest on empirical reality and prove to be rationally and "empirically" well-founded. He wished to demonstrate that Christian theology is not based on unprovable postulates; it rather has reason and experience on its side, because God bears testimony of himself to human reason not detached from knowable reality but in and through the world of experience!

As in his New Testament theology, in his dogmatics Schlatter sought to surmount false alternatives. At junctures "where otherwise contradictions broke thoughts into pieces and tore the will into tatters, I saw unities. Not nature alone, and not Christ alone, but both stood before me as God's work. Thus I had neither a mere nature-theology nor a mere Christ-theology but both. I was neither individualist nor socialist; I rather saw that we receive our personal life through community and community through our personal life. I was reminded of God not solely through the leading of destiny and not solely through inner enlivening; my faith received its content through both. . . . I did not concede that solely our mind is turned from Jesus to God, and neither did I grant that solely our will is made obedient to him, but saw that his grace grips us completely and gives to our minds certainty through his truth, just as it gives to our love purity through his righteousness. I no longer possessed, therefore, a doctrine dominated either by faith alone or by love alone. Rather, in faith I received love through Jesus' word."

In his dogmatics Schlatter concretized the fundamental theological concern that had accompanied him since his encounter with J. T. Beck: the positive coordination of complementary truths that are often torn asunder in theology, though closely intertwined in Holy Scripture. Thus Schlatter's dogmatics panoramically unfolded the deep unity of creation *and* redemption, nature *and* grace, law *and* gospel, justification *and* sanctification, faith *and* love, faith *and* understanding, revelation *and* reason. Even theologians with views similar to his were astonished at how Schlatter did not hesitate to employ unusual formulations, as for example when he took up (albeit in quite independent fashion) and furthered the traditional proofs for the existence of God. These had been widely endorsed in Protestant theology until the eighteenth century but since Kant had been generally regarded as discredited.

Regarded as a whole Schlatter's dogmatics attracted intense interest from others in the discipline since it could not be facilely placed into any one dogmatic school due to its independence but challenged *all* theological trajectories of the day. Church historian and Harnack student Karl Holl wrote to Schlatter excitedly, "Your book corresponds exactly to what I want to see in a dogmatics" (April 2, 1911). Holl was fascinated by how Schlatter could combine loyalty to dogmatic tradition in the foundational statements of the faith with intensive interaction with the questions raised by modernity: "Your work is modern in the best sense of the word and at the same time is not shy about placing time-tested simple principles, on which our conviction safely rests, before the reader" (ibid.). Schlatter's dogmatics likewise effectively confronted the supposition that a Bible-oriented theology must necessarily interfere with the freedom and breadth of intellectual labor.

After his dogmatics appeared Schlatter was urged by Karl Holl, but also by students, to produce an ethics, too, now that he had succeeded at presenting a complete synthesis of his theology. Holl had urgently admonished Schlatter not to evade this important task: "What kind of ethics is it, anyway, that modern Protestantism is following? . . . It is my firm conviction that the necessary starting point of Protestant renewal is its ethics; otherwise it will come to ruin. If I could, I would like to say to you what Farel said to Calvin: you will be guilty of the very weightiest sin of omission if you evade this obligation" (January 17, 1913).

Despite initial resistance to the idea, Schlatter decided to grant the request. It became "the little book that gave me the greatest joy." In its some four hundred pages Schlatter attempted to unfold a Christian ethics that arose consistently from the understanding of God's being and work presented in his dogmatics. He also sought to combine the indispensable inner orientation toward Scripture with the greatest possible interface with contemporary life and issues. Published in 1914 as World War I was breaking out, his *Die christliche Ethik* (*Christian Ethics*) was marked first by a comprehensive application of the New Testament. But it also distinguished itself by an unusually concrete discussion of ethical questions. It not only handled the traditional set themes of Protestant ethics (like the place of the Christian in marriage, family, state, and society); it also took up complexes of questions in a way that was unusual at the time: the moral regulation of criminal law, the relation of churches to each other, mission activity, the institutions of education and the press, medicine, art, and recreation, to name just a few. Schlatter's ethics was distinctive not only in the way it connected real life with biblical authority, but also in its affirmation of the idea of natural law and its linkage of a universally binding creation ethic with a specifically Christian discipleship ethic.

Schlatter's ethics became a perennial favorite of nontheologians (e.g., politicians) because of its extraordinary concreteness. For example, fifty years after it was published it was praised in the medical journal *Deutsches Ärzteblatt* as a "modern," "timelessly applicable" work! But Schlatter's investigation also raised intense interest in the field of scientific theology. Lutheran systematician Paul Althaus called it "the most practical, comprehensive ethics" that German Protestant theology had produced prior to Emil Brunner's renowned study *Das Gebot und die Ordnungen* in 1932.

With publication of his ethics Schlatter had reached his goal of ensuring that a summary of his exegetical and systematic insights would survive his death. To the four large volumes consisting of his New Testament theology, his dogmatics, and his ethics, in 1910 he completed his running interpretation of the whole New Testament in ten volumes. Called *Erläuterungen zum Neuen Testament* (*Explication of the New Testament*), it would eventually become a virtual classic, aiding generations of clergy and theologically inclined lay readers in gaining a deeper understanding of Scripture. In the seven years following his wife's death, Schlatter managed a published output of over four thousand pages—in addition to his academic teaching responsibilities!

This most productive phase in Schlatter's theological work was harshly terminated by the outbreak of World War I. Schlatter was inwardly prepared for a war, "for the danger that threatened us through France's tie with Russia became more visible with every passing summer." But Schlatter had not reckoned with a *World* War: in the hope that England would not take part in a war, he was willing "in the last days of July 1914 for one of my daughters to journey to Edinburgh to visit the missions seminar." The result was "that when she disembarked in Scotland, England had declared war." Schlatter had observed with mixed feelings the close alliance between imperial Germany and the Austrian monarchy. But in spite of such misgivings, like most Germans at the time he was willing to lend his support to Germany's entrance into the war.

Schlatter's son, Paul, was inducted into military service at the beginning of August 1914. He had just begun doctoral research in history on Napoleon. Two months later he was fatally wounded by a shell fragment. Schlatter claimed the body of his son at the military hospital in Germersheim and traveled with the coffin back to Tübingen. He was gripped by "the grimness of death, and I agonized for a long time, until the word of Jesus penetrated my soul: 'Lazarus, our friend, is asleep.'" On the train that night Schlatter scrawled on the cross on the coffin the words, "None of us lives for himself" (Rom. 14:7). His son, Theodor, reports that in response to yet another family death in the span of just a few years, Schlatter also "spoke a humble, courageous 'yes' of acceptance without any murmuring." Schlatter himself would later write, "The thought that I had suffered injustice never occurred to me." Yet Schlatter suffered grievously, not only over the loss of his son but also over the massive mortality levels on the battlefield, which exceeded all estimates more and more the longer the war went on. "Each night the oppressive awareness of death caused by the immense number of casualties settled on my soul, too."

Serious depression plagued Schlatter, causing him physical as well as emotional problems: the year after his son's death was characterized by a despondency and paralysis totally unprecedented in his life. His friend and colleague Theodor Häring seriously feared that Schlatter might have to terminate his teaching activity prematurely. He advised him to overcome his "aversion to visiting a doctor" (letter to Schlatter, March 14, 1915) and to take a semester break lest his feebleness persist (July 30, 1915).

In spite of his malaise Schlatter still found strength in July 1915 to compose a treatise on metaphysics at the request of the Hungarian Lutheran dogmatician Károly Pröhle. Its aim was to summarize his basic philosophical convictions. Certainly the most difficult and abstract of his works, it embodied Schlatter's attempt to unfold a metaphysic appropriate to the Christian faith. He was convinced that the revelation of Christ had, or should have, placed philosophical thinking, too, on a new foundation. This means that pre-Christian Greek philosophy ought to be subjected to a more comprehensive critique than has yet occurred in Christendom. Schlatter understood his *Metaphysik* as a contribution to the task of freeing theology from the foreign domination of pre-Christian philosophy, which in his view had manifested itself to an unduly strong degree in German idealism.

Wilhelm Lütgert was so taken with Schlatter's *Metaphysik* that he pressed Schlatter urgently to publish it in enlarged and, in a few places, improved form as the crowning touch to the summary of his thought represented in his New Testament theology, dogmatics, and ethics. Lütgert wrote to Schlatter (September 26, 1915), "My overall judgment is that you *must* allow your metaphysics to be published. It is necessary for an understanding of your dogmatics and your theology generally. It is therefore incumbent on you to do this." Yet Schlatter could not bring himself to make and follow through on this decision due to his depression, which made all he had written previously seem questionable to him. In his reply to Lütgert he lamented that much "[lies] on me, debilitating me: loneliness; the weight of war; lack of the motivation that teaching offers; memories of the innumerable dead, each of whom took a little piece of my life's work to the grave. . . . For the first time since entering the academic world I am experiencing the total stillness of idleness. . . . The future is shrouded in darkness. It is autumn for me; I'm a wilting leaf falling; whether in the meantime I will yet produce fruit remains uncertain. . . . I already close my eyes, full of pain, at the frightful series of books that I have been guilty of writing. One [truly good book] would have outweighed this whole miserable pile, each of which languishes unfinished, hardly begun" (October 18, 1915). It would be over seventy years before Schlatter's *Metaphysik* would become accessible to the public in 1987.

Luckily Schlatter's depression of 1914–15 did not last for the whole duration of the war. And yet the number and scope of his publications during the war show how cripplingly the war events affected his productivity: from 1914 to 1918 he published mainly only shorter essays, biblical expositions, and sermons. He did, however, manage to edit a brief summary of his theology, published in 1917 as *Die Gründe der christlichen Gewissheit* (*The Grounds of Christian Certainty*). He also wrote the treatise *Luthers Deutung des Römerbriefs* (*Luther's Interpretation of Romans*) in 1917, which was well received among specialists; a church-historical study entitled *Der Märtyrer in den Anfängen der Kirche* (*The Martyr in the Beginnings of the Church*) in 1915; and an exegetical study *Die beiden Schwerter* (*The Two Swords*) in 1916.

The events of the war did not compel Schlatter to make major changes in his theology. He had never endorsed the

45. Conflans, France, an important staging area for German troops in World War I. Schlatter (right of center) gave lectures to troops near the front.

shallow culture-Protestantism that became so popular in the final years of prewar Germany. That theology now lay in ruins in view of the almost apocalyptic dimensions of the Great War. Schlatter's theology, in contrast, drawn from the depths of Scripture, provided students not only resources for life but also for death. No one can calculate how many students during the war had the experience described by a soldier at the front who wrote to Karl Holl: "Intellectually and spiritually I am upheld by what I learned from Schlatter . . . ; for what he gave me still shines brightly even in the most frightful peril of death."

Schlatter was deeply shaken by the outcome of the war. He came to realize, of course, that Germany would not win the victory it had hoped. But he had not reckoned with such a decisive defeat, such a revolutionary political change from an imperial monarchy to a republic, and such harsh terms of peace. Schlatter was particularly disturbed by the ghastly high death counts of modern war along with its terrible effects on the civilian population. In fact, after the war ended he subjected the chapter entitled "War" in his ethics to a thoroughgoing revision. Without calling in question a state's right to military self-defense, he now argued that "modern war should no longer be viewed as one of the normal means of conducting politics." With the rise of new technologies, war's unprecedented destructiveness to combatants was painfully obvious, "to say nothing of the physical devastation that modern war brought to civilians, the moral defilement that it produced, and the bloodthirstiness and destructive fury that it encouraged." The traditional view that war was simply an alternative means of furthering political ends was shattered for Schlatter by the experience of the First World War, although this did not cause him to find a moral alternative in a doctrine of pacifism.

Schlatter felt that the collapse of the imperial government was "divine judgment" on Germany, yet at the same time "divine grace": "The outcome smashed our illusions and precisely thereby became a rich blessing. For the destruction of our illusions is a work of divine grace. . . . I remind myself . . . with burning regret that I, too, required the terrible events of 1914–18 so that my participation in our nation would be moderated by the fervor of repentance."

Based on this outlook Schlatter, in contrast to many of his contemporaries and colleagues, could accept the fall of the imperial monarchy as providential. He endorsed the new democratic political order, since with his Swiss background he had never felt a close tie to the deposed Hohenzollern dynasty. The same could not be said for many Protestant Christians in Germany, in whom "faithfulness to the king" had been instilled from their childhood. But Schlatter saw opportunities in the new political order that would have been unthinkable formerly. For example, the separation of church and state that the new republican structure brought with it fulfilled a desire that Schlatter had long harbored but did not expect to see fulfilled in his lifetime. His understanding of history affirmed that "the flexibility of history . . . is directed by the divine government" and that a political ethic must prove itself in the "comprehension of the historically possible." This protected Schlatter from whining lament for the monarchical state. And he had possessed a sharp eye for the weaknesses of the last German kaiser anyway.

Overall, the death of his son and the sorrowful wane of the German empire during the war (and in the years thereafter) brought Schlatter to identify "to the ultimate depths" (Theodor Schlatter) with the fate of the German people. Although Swiss, he carried a German passport and increasingly lost the status of *Ausländer* (foreigner). On the basis of his theology he could recognize patterns of divine grace and mercy even in Germany's baleful experiences. Characteristic here is his reminiscence regarding the disastrous inflation of 1923: "[I] can only be thankful for that which the so-called 'inflation' brought to me. [For it] gave me . . . a new view into the glory of Jesus. . . . In all honesty, before that time his word about 'treasure in heaven,' which makes the poor rich [cf. Luke 12:34], remained opaque to me. . . . Now the visible harvest of my work was swept away, and I retained nothing more than what Jesus had called treasure in heaven, God's grace and what it bestows on our lives. From that point on I presented the Sermon on the Mount with a cleaner conscience than previously."

On August 16, 1922, on his seventieth birthday, Schlatter was relieved of his academic obligations. But in view of his unusual mental and physical vitality and the large numbers of students wishing to learn from him, he exercised his right to offer academic lectures for eight more years, until the winter semester of 1929–30.

In his three decades at Tübingen Schlatter exerted an intellectual and spiritual influence that can barely be gauged. Students streamed to Tübingen from both Germany and elsewhere to hear him, so that at times his lectures were attended by more than six hundred. For many these lectures became a fascinating experience: "The professor [i.e., Schlatter] entered the lecture hall briskly, waving an unpretentious-looking slip of paper in the direction of the lengthy applause, looking somehow aggressive and unconventional, cheerful and interested in us young people. When the applause subsided he went immediately to his work" (Hans Stroh). Schlatter impressed the students not only by the content of what he said but also by his tremendously lively lecture style, almost totally free from notes: "I showed the young people that came to me how I dealt with the text, placed myself before them as an example and lent them my eyes so that they learned to see. . . . For me everything was focused on the productiveness of the hour that we had been given to be together. Therefore I spoke without notes."

Entirely in keeping with his conviction that true exegesis consists in the act of "seeing what is there," the goal of Schlatter's New Testament lectures was to lead his students to the point of *seeing*—apprehending truly the New Testament's

46. 1927

statements commensurate with philological, historical, theological, and personal considerations. Not a few hearers learned by personal experience how in Schlatter's lectures the scientific "act of seeing" became a direct address to personal existence. The word of Scripture, truly apprehended, disclosed a spiritual force that placed the hearer directly before God himself: "Among those things that remain unforgettable in the minds of all who were privileged to get to know [Schlatter] is this: again and again the lecture hall was transformed into a worship sanctuary, without Schlatter employing any kind of liturgical or pseudo-liturgical devices whatsoever" (Karl Heinrich Rengstorf). Schlatter taught in the confidence that "when we read the New Testament we" turn "our ears to the most content-rich and powerful Word . . . that has ever been uttered, to that Word that gives us the promise: here God reveals himself to us."

Therefore, Schlatter saw "opening up the Scriptures" his "primary concern" during all the years of his teaching min-

47. Karl Barth, 1966

48. Emil Brunner

istry. He was convinced that treatment of dogmatic and ethical themes could only be beneficial when the foundational act of listening to the Scriptures was not minimized or set aside. One of the most fruitful effects of Schlatter's academic work may have been that he guided and educated countless hearers in committed listening to the Scriptures.

Adolf Schlatter

Schlatter's foremost concern of introducing his students as comprehensively as possible to the entire wealth of the New Testament caused him to devote less and less time to teaching systematics as years went by at Tübingen. Apart from three introductory courses in theology and the "Creation and Redemption" course in the summer semester of 1922, Schlatter gave nothing but New Testament lectures after the beginning of World War I. He continued to follow developments in the area of systematic theology with careful scrutiny, but he left public interaction in the areas of dogmatics and ethics largely to younger friends, among whom Wilhelm Lütgert would be primary.

Nevertheless, he did concern himself in notable fashion with discussion concerning dialectical theology as it increasingly came to occupy center stage in the 1920s. This theology sought to move beyond "nineteenth-century theology" through determined reflection on the witness of the Bible and the Reformation. Schlatter's interest was attracted especially to Karl Barth (1886–1968) and Emil Brunner (1889–1966). On the one hand, Schlatter thought early dialectical theology was hampered by serious attenuations of the witness of Scripture. For example, Schlatter criticized its insufficient attention to creation and nature, its neglect of the doctrine of the Holy Spirit and of ethics, its irrational detaching of faith from knowledge, and a too restricted understanding of revelation. On the other hand, he took it seriously as a discussion partner whose criticism of "nineteenth-century theology" he expressly shared at a number of points. For example, like the dialectical theologians Schlatter rejected Schleiermacher's man-centered theology as well as the bourgeois culture-Protestantism that dominated Germany prior to the First World War. And Schlatter supported dialectical theology's energetic reflection on Scripture and the Reformers.

In 1922 Schlatter took up the pen to comment on the second edition of Barth's famous Romans commentary. He valued the "power" of Barth's interpretation, but he lamented its ahistorical tone, subjectiveness, and irrationality. To initiate a fruitful interchange with Barth, he put Barth's name forward in 1924 and 1926 to be a speaker at the Bethel theological conferences. Unfortunately Barth could not comply with this request. Yet Schlatter's invitation of 1924 inaugurated a letter exchange between the two Swiss theologians that continued until 1936. Mutual respectful esteem marked their correspondence. In view of the considerable theological differences between Schlatter and Barth and the sharpness of theological interchange in that setting, this exchange is a fine testimony to how a truly Christian dialogue emphasizing common ground and fairness can be carried on even when there are deep-seated differences in theological approach.

Schlatter and Barth managed good-willed interaction via letter but arrived at no agreement in the theological questions at issue. Things were different between Schlatter and Emil Brunner. From the end of the 1920s onward they grew closer as Brunner and Barth drifted progressively further apart. In 1929 Brunner wrote to Schlatter, "I have learned much from you and in a roundabout way am coming closer and closer to your views." And in 1934, the year when a decisive break between Barth and Brunner occurred, Brunner confessed in a letter to Schlatter, "Without wanting to, and sometimes without realizing it at the time, I came nearer to your position step by step. I was surprised how, in the measure that I turned independently to the New Testament, I concurred there with you" (December 8, 1934). In that year's dispute between Barth and Brunner over the question of a knowable revelation through creation Schlatter came out unambiguously on Brunner's side, since in Schlatter's view the New Testament (Rom. 1:19f. and elsewhere) testifies beyond doubt to the reality of a self-disclosure of God that touches all persons.

It would be a mistake to regard Schlatter's effectiveness in Tübingen from a theological-scientific point of view only, for his activity also had a pastoral dimension that should not be

Adolf Schlatter

49. With son Theodor during the Bethel "Theological Week,"
September 26, 1926

underestimated. Alongside his lectures and seminars he spent
an extraordinary amount of time with his students. He was
available to them daily in the early afternoon for talks of a
personal or pastoral nature. Here in the privacy of personal
interaction "momentous decisions in great number" were
made (Karl Heinrich Rengstorf).

In addition, each Monday evening students from any field
of study were invited to an "open evening." Anyone interested
could attend without prior notice. Pastor Gustav Heidenreich
offers this reminiscence: "At quarter after eight he entered the
room, cigar box under his arm. He shook each person's hand,
then took his seat at the table and eyed each guest. . . . The proceedings often became lively. Everyone could speak his mind.

And if a student blurted out something that was foolish, there was no fear of biting criticism or insult. Schlatter must have often smiled at what came forth from the students' hearts, but he was polite and kind and so smiled to himself, never wounding whoever had spoken. He took the young men and women seriously, and for that reason they also took him seriously. . . . Whatever Schlatter spoke about, his hearers gained the impression that [for Schlatter] faith and life were indissolubly linked. . . . From some 'open evenings' at Schlatter's house we returned home just as blessed as we would have felt upon leaving a lecture or God's house after a sermon. Schlatter was always outstanding, because he breathed the air of eternity."

Together with Karl Heim, Schlatter had a strong influence on a Tübingen group called the German Christian Student Union (GCSU). He served them over the course of many years as Bible teacher and advisor. Since Tübingen was the GCSU center for Christian students of all majors, Schlatter gained great influence in the organization everywhere in Germany after his Tübingen years got underway. He shaped its "direction and character . . . in special measure" (Wilhelm Lütgert), since he repeatedly addressed well-attended transregional student conferences (e.g., the Freudenstädter Tagungen) and published often in *Die Furche*, the official organ of the GCSU. Thus Schlatter was able to exert considerable influence, not only on pastors-in-training, but also on Christian academicians throughout Germany.

In summary, Adolf Schlatter was not only a theological teacher for his students but also a shepherd and counselor. His profound, often life-changing influence on students bears out the truth of the saying that he often repeated, "We move each other more powerfully by what we do than by what we say." Rudolf Brezger characterized the spiritual-personal dimension of Schlatter's effect on his own life as follows: "Adolf Schlatter lived his theology, a theology of joy and of thanks. Word and life were a tangible unity. When he stood before students or in the pulpit, joy radiated from his eyes.

50. With Grandson Theodor (1928)

You could see that he was moved by joy in the Lord in all his work. . . . Adolf Schlatter shared with his students that which was most personal to him, his faith, his prayer, his thinking, his praise of God. The manner that he led them in communion at the Lord's Table left the bright memory of a noble festive occasion. Our fellowship with him formed and strengthened our faith in the Holy Spirit."

51. At a Swiss pastors' conference in Zurich, April 19–20, 1927. Schlatter is seated; standing (left) are the blind New Testament scholar Eduard Riggenbach and Old Testament scholar Walther Eichrodt (center).

It may be counted as one of the distinctives of Schlatter's impact that he was concerned to an extraordinary degree to serve the Christian community outside the academic sphere, not merely within it. Among his many-sided activities, for example, were numerous years of service as chair of Tübingen's Young Men's Christian Association (YMCA). In his capacity as YMCA chairman Schlatter studied the Bible, not only with laborers, business people, and new believers, but also with YMCA members in the interest of improving their general knowledge. Especially memorable remain those evenings when Schlatter drew on his broad botanical knowledge to lead his hearers into the wonders of the plant world.

52. At a ladies Bible circle meeting, 1930

Wherever his services were requested Schlatter made himself available. The Tübingen YMCA could count on him, as could the Protestant youth ministry among young women in the Tübingen area or the ladies' circle for whom Schlatter led a Bible study in his living room until he was eighty-six years old. With this last-named group Schlatter covered nearly the whole of the New Testament. It also bears mention that until 1929 Schlatter conducted monthly worship services in the Tübingen university church, where he also served on the church council.

Schlatter's Tübingen sermons were well liked by those who heard them and widely read in printed form. He placed a high priority on his preaching ministry: "When I reflect on what brought me to Tübingen, and then imagine what not serving the university church would have meant, I know I would have regarded it as a major loss." His sermons were marked by exposition that was both strictly text-centered and original. His vigorous language avoided all rhetorical embellishments. His preaching was profoundly Protestant in its strong emphasis on justification through grace alone. By means of its emphatic focus on repentance, love, and response, however, his sermons led beyond an attenuated understanding of Reformation theology into the breadth of the biblical message.

Many hearers never forgot Schlatter's spiritual radiance as he preached. This offset the difficulty that some had in understanding him due to his St. Gallen dialect. Theodor Brandt said, "A wonderful joy and assurance permeated the preacher's testimony." Thomas Breit recalled, "[In his preaching] he did not always make it easy for the congregation. He often led us along paths of profound mental challenge, speaking with such gusto that at times we could barely follow. . . . Yet at times the church building could hardly hold the crowds that streamed into it. . . . At times it seemed to us as if the glow of another world would shine roundabout his head. The words he spoke in the church carried an authority that always made us take notice."

In Tübingen Schlatter was active not only in church and Christian work but also in the social-political arena. Together with Martin Haug, who later became bishop of that German state, and the Tübingen systematician Karl Heim, Schlatter publicly supported the *Christlicher Volksdienst* (Christian Public Service Party) at its founding in 1924 (in 1929 it became the Christian-Social Public Service Party [hereafter C-SPSP]). This group consisted of Pietist Christians of both the state church and independent churches who sought a democratic and socially responsible political order based on Christian principles.

In Schlatter's view the acceptance of political responsibility was a labor of love for church and society that Christen-

53. 450th anniversary of the University of Tübingen, July 25, 1927. Festive procession of professors includes Karl Müller (third from right), Karl Heim (fourth from right), Schlatter (seventh from right).

dom could not rightly evade. For that reason he did not hesitate to support the Christian Public Service Party with his counsel and public statements. In 1927 he published a speech entitled "Christendom's Participation in the Formation of Our National Character" in a Christian Public Service Party publication. It reads like a prophetic warning of the coming Nazi Führer-cult when in this speech Schlatter laments that Germans "suffer from a deluded political Führer-fixation." This political outlook "seeks to order the state . . . from the top down in a highly centralized fashion, with the result that the central leadership suppresses and cripples the vital members of the nation."

In another speech given in Tübingen for the same party on February 18, 1929 ("What Does Our Nation's Situation Require from Its Protestant Christendom?"), Schlatter em-

54. With son Theodor, September 1, 1929, at work on indexes for the third edition of Schlatter's *Die christliche Ethik*

Adolf Schlatter

55. With daughter Dora, who in his later years read to him aloud, September 1, 1929

phasized the necessity of a "Protestant politics." It would have to overcome the equating of "Christendom" with "conservatism" and "middle-class" bourgeois society. At the same time Schlatter spoke positively regarding the (predominantly Catholic) *Deutsche Zentrumspartei* (German Centrist Party), to which Protestant Christians owed a great deal. When the C-SPSP all at once received fourteen mandates and nearly nine hundred thousand votes in the parliamentary election of 1930, a surprisingly fruitful cooperation got underway with the German Centrist Party, especially in areas of shared Christian concern. This joint work helped prevent the collapse of Brüning's cabinet for about two years. Starting in 1930 Schlatter's party was also one of the few groups who, with unduped clarity of vision, warned of the dangerous threat posed by National Socialism (the Nazis).

Yet many Protestant Christians could not bring themselves to support the C-SPSP, instead preferring the *Deutschnational Partei* (German National Party) and finally the Nazi Party itself. When Paul Bausch, C-SPSP parliamentary representative during both Third Reich and Federal Republic of Germany regimes, surveyed those years, he commented: "If all leading men of the Protestant church had thought as clearly as Schlatter did, the fate of the German people would probably have turned out different." But too many Protestants were inclined to support the Nazi movement.

When Schlatter finally ceased academic teaching after his one hundredth semester (winter term 1929–30), he did not enter a phase of repose and relaxation. It rather marked the start of a segment of life highlighting his scientific produc-

56. Spring 1930 in the yard of Schlatter's Tübingen residence

57. In old age

tivity in truly astonishing fashion. In just eight years (1929–37) he published one after another of his nine now-famous scientific commentaries on Matthew (1929), John (1930), Luke (1931), James (1932), the Corinthian letters (1934), Mark (1935), Romans (1935), the Pastoral letters (1936), and 1 Peter (1937). Of these commentaries, filling more than four thousand pages, the most significant are perhaps the ones on Matthew, Romans, Corinthians, and James. Altogether they have undergone more than thirty printings so far, assuring Schlatter's place as one of the greatest New Testament scholars of the twentieth century—indeed, one of the truly great Scripture interpreters in the history of Christendom!

Schlatter's commentaries are marked once more by that knack for synthesis which was the hallmark of his Scripture interpretation throughout his life. Joachim Jeremias termed it "the connection of philological exactitude and profound theological exegesis."

In those politically and theologically portentous years of Weimar disintegration and Nazi ascent, Schlatter's scientific exposition of the New Testament was received by many theologians of various stripes as very beneficial reflection on those spiritual foundations for theology and church with which every era must come to grips. Thus Karl Barth wrote to him (May 2, 1934): I "may . . . tell you—certainly speaking for many—how thankful we are to know that you are so vigorously at work on the very front lines (for that is what Scripture exposition is), and to be able to participate again and again in the fruits of your experiences and efforts."

It is simply astounding that in spite of his great age Schlatter's output far exceeded just these nine commentaries. Between 1929 and 1937 he wrote nearly ninety additional publications, among them his translation of the New Testament and his magisterial *Theologie des Judentums nach dem Bericht des Josefus* (*The Theology of Judaism Based on Josephus' Accounts*).

Schlatter was an unusually energetic person, but this productivity was possible only because of great persistence in his labors. Gertrud Schoppen, who resided in the same house as Schlatter during the last years of his life, gives a vivid depiction of this last great phase of work: "The amount of work performed in the stillness of his study was prodigious. Once I was sick and spent several weeks abed in the room that lay next to where he did his work. I thus became aware of his habits at close range. What struck me most was this great persistence in his work. In the morning between seven and eight o'clock he entered the room. Then his breakfast was

58. In 1932

brought to him. Next the workday began, sometimes prefaced by a short time of singing. I always wondered whether these were psalms! I could not make out what he sang, but the tone of praise and worship came through strongly. At a later point there would be a short break for a cup of hot chocolate, after which work resumed until lunch. A bell would sound, and he would respond immediately. Lunch was followed by a short rest period, then a cup of milk along with the newspaper, which one of his daughters read aloud to him in his last years. After this his work claimed his full attention again until supper. This set pattern was seldom broken, and even then only in the case of visitors. And thus he managed to fill thousands of pages with his clear handwriting." Schlatter's enormous output in the last eight years of his long life is all the more remarkable when one considers that he did not pull back into an ivory tower of scholarly isolation but continued to take active part in the dynamic political and ecclesiastical events of those tumultuous years.

As supporter of the *Christlicher Volksdienst* (Christian Public Service Party) Schlatter followed with concern the strengthening of the Nazi Party at the end of the Weimar years. Already in 1931 he commented critically on the view of man and ethic of the National Socialist (Nazi) movement. The most that the church could expect from them, he opined, would be "well-intentioned tolerance" (letter to his son, Theodor, February 8, 1931). After Hitler forcibly seized power in January 1933, Schlatter's fears grew increasingly strong. He bemoaned the "strangulation of the [German] parliament" that resulted from the Act of Enablement (March 24, 1933) and the disregard for the existing legal order by the "almighty" Nazis: "They have assumed a power that no one in Germany ever possessed until now" (April 2, 1933). He was especially troubled by the militarization of the German populace and the way it was being "trained and nurtured for war" (May 7, 1933). For the church Schlatter feared the worst: in June 1933 he expressed the concern that the "fate of Russia" would befall German Christendom, which was about to endure "a course of severe suffering" (June 26, 1933). He feared a church that would be totally conformed to the state, "a so-called church . . . whose role would be to work with the state and for its interests" and which would amount to little "more than window dressing" (June 26, 1933).

Adolf Schlatter

In contrast to many of his colleagues on the theological faculty, Schlatter observed National Socialist politics with unconcealed aloofness: "no one can accuse me of any kind of accommodation whatsoever" (October 15, 1933). He emphatically opposed the attempt of the so-called *Deutsche Christen* (German Christians) to create a "truly appropriate" theology and church tailor-made to the National Socialist state. In his essay "Die neue deutsche Art in der Kirche" ("The New German Behavior in the Church"), published in October 1933 against the counsel of his colleague Gerhard Kittel, he criticized the "German Christians" just as sharply as the Führer-cult and totalitarian demands of the National Socialist state: "No living community can be formed from people who are inwardly dead. No Führer can make a German paradise out of withered fig trees."

For Schlatter there was no question that the church was called to resistance in view of Nazi policy toward it. With respect to the form of church resistance, however, he called for a more careful approach than the *Bekennende Kirche* (Confessing Church). He supported the combining of resistance and conformity to the prevailing powers called for by the Protestant church leadership of the German state of Württemberg under Bishop Theophil Wurm. In view of his age (he was eighty when Hitler seized power) Schlatter curtailed his public statements about the political and church situation after 1933, concentrating entirely on his theological work. The attentive observer, however, has no difficulty detecting (especially in his Corinthians commentary) how firmly Schlatter kept his own times before his eyes, even in his theological publications. He addressed at least indirectly the ecclesiastical and political situation that surrounded him.

There was one more instance when Schlatter felt himself constrained to address the German public with a direct appeal. This was a piece published at Christmas in 1935—and confiscated by the Gestapo. Its title was "Wird der Jude über uns siegen?" ("Will the Jew Be Victorious over Us?"). In

59. Schlatter's desk in the month of his death, May 1938

it Schlatter sharply criticized the neo-pagan propaganda favored by the Nazis with their crass racism. With prophetic clarity of vision Schlatter expressed the fear that the "victory of our race over all other peoples" called for by the Nazis would be bought at the price of "a battlefield . . . full of corpses and devastation." The value of Schlatter's brave polemic was weakened, however, by his failure to speak up for the German Jewish Party, which was at that time already at a severe disadvantage due to repressive legal measures. Schlatter did not recognize the danger that threatened the Jews.

Schlatter's most significant utterance regarding the political and ecclesiastical situation in the Third Reich may be his last work, a devotional volume provocatively entitled *Kennen wir Jesus?* (*Do We Know Jesus?*). Schlatter penned this book—which sold forty thousand copies while he was still alive!—out of deep concern for what lay ahead for the German people, whom he saw in grave danger because of National Socialist anti-Christianity. In 366 devotional essays he sought one last time to portray Jesus Christ for his read-

151

ership in a penetrating fashion. Christ, Schlatter tried to show, is the sole sufficient foundation for the life of the individual and the nation.

After this book appeared the eighty-five-year-old man's strength perceptibly waned. He could no longer work at his desk and spent his days on an old reclining chair. Schlatter had been healthy his whole life. He did not remember having spent even one day in bed. Now, however, a heart problem grew increasingly evident. Eventually shortness of breath developed as well. "In the last months he repeatedly asked that his own works be read to him, testing whether they stood up to scrutiny so near to eternity" (Gertrud Schoppen). His

60. In old age

thoughts turned increasingly to the age to come: "In calm confidence he waited for the homegoing" (Theodor Schlatter). On the morning of May 19, 1938, for the first time in his life, he could no longer stand up. Shortly after eleven he died without death throes, "quietly and peacefully."

A life had ended that was dedicated entirely to biblical renewal of theology and church. His death was felt by many as the loss of not only a great "teacher of the church" (the title of one commemorative volume that appeared in 1938) but also a "father in Christ" (title of another, 1939). Not a few persons owed to Schlatter decisive influence for good in their lives. Bodelschwingh Jr. spoke for many when he stated at Schlatter's interment: "For me personally and for many others he became a leader to Christ. He opened up for us the most intimate aspects of the language of the New Testament. He showed us what it means to serve the church. Always, whenever we thought of him, there stood before us the picture of a man who had grown free and fruitful because God's gospel lived in him."

Select Bibliography

Below is a selection of the primary sources used in this biography. Unpublished items are in the Schlatter archives in Stuttgart, Germany. Asterisked items (*) are autobiographical. For a more comprehensive list of Schlatter's writings and related secondary literature (all in German), see Werner Neuer, *Adolf Schlatter* (Wuppertal: Brockhaus, 1988), pp. 181–86.

I. Unpublished sources, with titles translated into English (archive number in parentheses)

*Adolf Schlatter: Life history for church overseers (#151)
*————: Obituary for deceased wife (#158)
*————: "Idealism and the revival during my youth" (#769)
————: Letters from student days to parents (#448)
————: Letters to son Theodor (#1229)
————: Letters to Friedrich Barth (#1234)
————: Letters to Wilhelm Lütgert (#421)
*————: Reports on pastoral experiences and times in Bern, Greifswald, and Berlin (#683)
Karl Barth: Letters to Adolf Schlatter (#425)
Adolf Bolliger: Letters to Adolf Schlatter (#425)
Emil Brunner: Letters to Adolf Schlatter (#425)
Theodor Häring: Letters to Adolf Schlatter (#426)
Martin Kähler: Letters to Adolf Schlatter (#426)
Theoderich von Lerber: Letters to Adolf Schlatter (#426)
Wilhelm Lütgert: Letters to Adolf Schlatter (#429)

Select Bibliography

Erich Schraeder: Letters to Adolf Schlatter (#427)
Paul Wurster: Letters to Adolf Schlatter (#427)

II. Published sources

*Schlatter, Adolf. "Adolf Schlatter." *Die Religionswissenschaft der Gegenwart in Selbstdarstellungen.* Vol. 1. Ed. by E. Stange. Leipzig, 1925. 145–69.

* ———. "Die Entstehung der *Beiträge zur Förderung christlicher Theologie* und ihr Zusammenhang mit meiner theologischen Arbeit zum Beginn ihres fünfundzwanzigsten Bandes." BFChTh 25/1, 1920.

* ———. *Erlebtes.* Berlin, [5]1929.

* ———. *Rückblick auf meine Lebensarbeit.* Stuttgart, [2]1977.

Appendix A

Key Dates and Events in Schlatter's Life

1852 (August 16)	Born in St. Gallen, Switzerland
1871–73	Study in Basle, Switzerland
1873–74	Study in Tübingen, Germany
1875	Exams in Basle
	Pastorate in Kilchberg, Switzerland
1875–76	Pastorate in Neumünster, Switzerland
1877–80	Pastorate in Kesswil, Switzerland
1880 (January 15)	Married to Susanna Schoop
1880	Called to Bern, Switzerland; *Habilitation*
1881–88	Lecturer in New Testament at Bern
1885	Publication of first monograph, the prize-winning *Der Glaube im Neuen Testament*
1888–93	Professor of New Testament in Greifswald, Germany

Appendix A

1893–98	Professor of systematic theology in Berlin, Germany
1897–	Editorship (with H. Cremer and later W. Lütgert) of *Beiträge zur Förderung christlicher Theologie*
1898–1922	Professor of New Testament in Tübingen, Germany
1907 (July 9)	Death of Susanna (Schoop) Schlatter
1914 (October 14)	Death of Schlatter's son, Paul
1909–14	Summarization of prior theological work in four volumes: *Das Wort Jesu* (1909), *Die Lehre der Apostel* (1910), *Das christliche Dogma* (1911), and *Die christliche Ethik* (1914)
1922 (August 16)	Release from academic duties (obligatory at age seventy)
1928	Final university seminar
1929–30	Final university lectures
1929–37	Compilation of exegetical life's work in nine large scientific New Testament commentaries treating Matthew (1929), John (1930), Luke (1931), James (1932), Corinthians (1934), Mark (1935), Romans (1935), Pastorals (1936), and 1 Peter (1937)
1937	Final large publication: *Kennen wir Jesus?*
1938 (May 19)	Death in Tübingen

Appendix B

Adolf Schlatter on Prayer[1]

Since prayer is that act by which we turn our will to God, prayer is of the very essence of religion. To be religious means to be capable of praying; to be irreligious means to be incapable of prayer. The struggle for religion is the struggle to pray; the theory of religion is the philosophy of prayer. Appropriate prayer is proper religion; corrupted prayer is debased religion. Prayer is the most direct expression of faith, because prayerfully turning our thoughts and will to God is the initial step from thought about God to full assurance of God. By the same token prayer is the most direct expression of love. It is an offering of highest priority, since the first thing we owe God is our thinking and willing.

Prayer involves gratitude, because we receive from God, and supplication, because we work for God. And since our work rests on God's work, adoration precedes both gratitude and supplication. It is through adoration that we come into line with what God is bringing to pass. It is essential for prayer that it does not merely focus on us and our concerns; it must rather be concerned with God's work and intention. Yet if we eradicated from our prayer the experiences that move us, we would not attain the form God intends for prayer to assume. Such eradication would be based on the idea that God puts up with no other life but his own. The purity of our love for

---

1. From Adolf Schlatter, Das christliche Dogma, 3rd ed. (Stuttgart: Calwer Verlag, 1977 [= 2nd ed., 1923]), pp. 203–212. Translated by Robert W. Yarbrough.

Appendix B

God is established by prayer that facilitates both access into ourselves and release from ourselves. It facilitates the former insofar as we prayerfully ground, purify, and confirm our will. It facilitates the latter insofar as we glimpse and appropriate God's work that extends beyond us and find in that work our goal and our joy.

The prayer that arises from our personal experience can dispense with neither gratitude nor supplication.

Through gratitude, our experience arrives at its intended goal for both our thinking and our willing. Gratitude ensures that we will properly assess what we experience, because when we are grateful we do not merely see the gift. Rather, through the gift we have regard for the giver. Or again, through gratitude we not only make sense of what happens to us; we also become mindful of the one who brought it to pass. An event that moves us to gratitude has become to us a revelation of God. To the extent we can give thanks, God in his working stands revealed to us. Gratitude is also the bulwark guarding our desiring from the ravages of unchecked selfishness. For it prevents us from exploiting what we receive for mere personal enhancement. In giving thanks we who receive and enjoy subordinate ourselves to him who bestows his largesse on us. And so it is that what goes forth from God attains its goal: It returns to him.

Prayer, however, as an activity required from us by God, involves not just thanks but also supplication. And supplication is a necessity, not simply when suffering threatens but also when duty and love call us to service. When we translate our designs for the future into supplication, they receive the same cleansing and deepening that gratitude confers on what we experience. Once more we are protected from the predations of selfish human will, since supplication implies that we forswear the arrogance of high-handed, independent acts. Rather, we form our wills before God. We bring our decisions for the future into submission under God. The ethical uprightness of our will, however, is also of greatest importance for the uprightness of our thinking, with which we formulate our thoughts about aims and goals.

Sometimes petition is denigrated in favor of thanksgiving. Behind this lies a concept of God that allows only for dependence and therefore hankers for a false ideal of piety in which human will disappears.[2] And supplication would, in fact, be an aberration if we had neither the liberty nor ability to will, neither the liberty nor ability to love. Giving grounds for

---

2. "The only place for the love of God to express itself is in love for the brethren" (Ritschl, Unterricht in der chr. Rel. §6). It followed naturally that Ritschl had an aversion against supplication (Rechtf. und Versöhnung, 3rd ed., 608). This aversion can be attributed to various factors working together: his dependence on Schleiermacher's concept of religion, his dependence on the Augsburg doctrine of faith, his polemic against Catholic piety, his criticism of Pietism with its push toward works and, as a result, its emphasis on supplicatory prayer. If it were the case, as religious tradition

concern about asking things from God in prayer is the fact that our wills
constantly tend to disfigure supplication. Prayer is often enough controlled
by egoistic greed concerned only for personal welfare. But we do not overcome our corrupt wills through exercising no will at all, nor our eudae-
monism through apathy. It is true that in the purity or impurity of our supplication there is direct reflection of the purity or impurity of our desire.
But that does not amount to an injunction to abandon supplication; on the
contrary, it amounts to proof that supplication is indispensable. For we
inevitably abandon the fight against our corrupt wills if we cease to measure our desires against God's will, nor base what we desire on what God
desires. But we do both to the extent that our desires become supplication.

Whoever has recognized that prayer is the right way of conduct also knows
that it is of greatest importance for the course of one's history. That which
orients us ethically brings a formative strength to bear on the things that hap-
pen to us. In that prayerlessness corrupts us, the absence of prayer inevitably
works woe in our history, too, all that we experience and do.

If we deny God our adoration, we turn our gaze and our yearning away
from his self-attestation. We block his work from view, thereby making it
fruitless for us. Now we are on the verge of striving against God's reign.
Ingratitude devalues the good things God entrusts us with and makes us
superficial. It thereby also affects our future, because the reception of subsequent gifts is based on the constructive use of previous ones. If we are
fruitless in our use of God's previously-granted bounty, we are not ready for
new gifts. Rather, we begin to lose even what was previously granted.

In conferring legitimacy on our wishes through supplication, what we
request can be carried out and fulfilled. We have God as an accomplice in
what we do, once we have prepared ourselves through prayer to be God's
accomplice. He who must act faces the choice of either praying or offend-
ing God, and he chooses the latter by determining his conduct
autonomously. Such conduct amounts to a negation of God. Supplication
is imperative for doing one's work as God's servant; every legitimate action
must be a fruit of prayer.

In prayer we run the risk of distorting the idea of God, because we pray
with an awareness of our own causal potential. This potential is at work in
every act of our will. Such distortion is averted if faith is the origin of our
prayer's inner resolve. Through faith prayer becomes subordinate to God.
Prayer achieves elevation to him only through our positioning beneath
God's kindness. We know that the value conferred on us by prayer is given

---

often claims, that suffering were the only ground given to us for supplication, then the
counsel might be plausible that we should replace supplication with surrender. However, we receive the will that we need for fulfillment not only through pain but through
the duty that is laid on us. And therefore we can no more do away with supplication
than we can do away with our occupations.

Appendix B

by God himself; we recognize that the active potential that prayer possesses is bestowed by God himself. He alone provides the right and privilege to worship, thank, and make request. Faith is God's gift; so too is that prayer that proceeds from faith. Precisely through believing prayer we overcome the arrogance that would gladly place itself above God. And humility becomes a possibility, for we receive with thanks all good things from his hand, as we derive with supplication our actions from his will. As faith brings about deliverance from the self, prayer brings about repudiation of our selfish will—not so that we will become will-less, but so that our will might be founded on God's rule and reign.

If our idea of God has the effect of making prayer impossible for us, what we have is resignation, not faith. We have thereby dispensed with God's love. In this conception God works only to constrict, not to free, only to absorb, not to enliven. No personalized relationship arises between him and us. Consequently, our conduct remains meaningless to him. But to consign man to nothingness in this way inevitably involves arrogance, since we remain persons who express our wills, despite all meditations on our nothingness. Only now we demand that God grant us what is good apart from prayer, that he carry out our will although we have neither entreated him nor given him thanks.

Currently a pressing difficulty is posed by the regularity of the natural order and the comprehensiveness of its causal connections. We hear the objection: "To offer supplication is to make the demand that God alter the course on which the world is set. Therefore prayer amounts to an act of world-negation, an attempt to sever, through our pleas, the law binding on us. All prayer presupposes an idea of miracle that is sheer fantasy." The decisive question here is whether we are capable of willing. Now if the natural process excludes the will, that not only does away with "request" as a category of human expression; it also renders human desiring in all its forms, including the religious form of prayer, self-deception. When the will is reduced to nothing but illusion, prayer meets the same fate. But when we give credence to what our consciousness tells us—that we do in fact have and exercise will—then we are certain that our will is a force to be reckoned with in the course that this world is taking. Then we also have the task of ordering our conduct rightly vis-à-vis that course. And "rightly" means that we commit our will to God. We abandon the notion of mastering the course of the world in any way, except as our desiring is confirmed, acted on, and fulfilled by God. In prayer we do not arrogate mastery of the world to ourselves; rather we know ourselves to be free before the world only through coming into like-mindedness with God.

The prayerless person, in contrast, is deluded, since he steadily demands that nature hark to his will, for no other reason than that he wants it to. He demands from the world and from others that they pay attention to his wishes, as if he were a force superior to the world. In spite of all theories that deny the will, we remain people who exercise it—and we therefore inevitably make requests. But we are not condemned to exert a godless will that focuses only on things and people and ignores God.

Yet every prayer moves beyond the concept of a closed-nexus world. After all, it addresses God, and it has an eye for far more than natural factors and their regular, naturally ordered outworking. Prayer always affirms the sovereignty of God. This is not to say, however, that prayer necessarily postulates miracle, or that it denies laws of nature. For the acknowledgment of God is also the acknowledgment of the world as the work of God, and of the laws of nature as something established by God. We do not pray against nature, for we call on him who gave nature its form and working mechanisms. In prayer we accept nature as it truly is. What we deny is only nature as it has come to be atheistically misconstrued, nature as that ugly specter said to exist and function without God, or in God's stead. Thus we are not asking for something unnatural, but for what is natural from the God through whom nature exists and thrives. We move beyond nature only in the sense that we direct our desiring to God, and we know that he possesses will and capacity that is inexhaustible. He dispenses gifts from a perfection that towers over all the limitations that hem in the natural processes.

Accordingly, the limits of prayer are not to be gained by calculation of the possibility of success. Rather the limits are purely internal to the faith of the one who prays. The extent of our right to pray is the extent to which faith reaches. Prayers forced beyond faith become sin. Now it is true that God's grace has the power to respond even to such prayers, however defiled, frightfully skeptical, or arrogantly demanding they may be. But the perfection of divine grace does not absolve us from the obligation of making our prayer pure—that is, of praying trustingly, not distrustfully. This obligation springs directly from the perfection of grace and from the perfect promise to answer prayer which that grace expresses. We depend on an unconditional pledge, and we have also received it from Jesus, because it is only an unconditional promise that suffices to bring us to faith. Conditional promises throw us back into uncertainty and doubt. But sure promise does not result in arbitrary, irresponsible exercise of prayer. Rather, the necessity of faith sets limits from within to what we ask for. For faith does not consist in some abstract, woolly thought hovering over our concrete concern. If that were the case, arbitrary expressions of prayer could hardly be avoided. Rather, we are bound to conduct ourselves believingly in the ordained relationships that form prayer's subject matter. Prayer calls for the certainty of God's response to what we ask for. And that in itself sets boundaries to prayer, because we cannot confer the certainty of faith on ourselves arbitrarily. We must be internally empowered to attain it. We

Appendix B

must be given the conviction that what we ask for is available to us in the divine goodness.

Here it must be pointed out that our certainty is always mingled with what we do not know, because faith lays hold of both the knowledge given to us, and the lack of knowledge appointed for us, with the same determination. We know him whom we address, but we do not yet see the deed by which he presently helps and endows us. What we do know is the comprehensive perfection of divine grace in its concrete relatedness to the state of our lives. What we do not know is the ways and means through which God will demonstrate the divine grace to us.

It is possible to separate from each other both the knowing and the not-knowing that constitute prayer. When we fancy ourselves as commanding full knowledge, so that in prayer we have the capacity to determine what God should do, then the consciousness of our distance from God is extinguished, God's superiority to us is obscured, and prayer transmutes to command—and so degenerates to arrogance. On the other hand, when we denigrate ourselves as knowing nothing, we have hidden and denied to ourselves God's goodness. Then, although that goodness testifies its presence to us, we do not apprehend it. Our consciousness assumes a dullness that amounts to guilt, because it implicitly disregards the divine goodness. Prayer becomes a quarrel with God, a reproach against him, an experiment that takes up the cudgels in an attempt to shake him awake and remind him of his duty.

The denial of prayer requests often and necessarily goes hand-in-hand with our praying. This is because prayer does not set its sights on naturally controlled effects; rather, it appeals to God, whose own will orders our life. We cannot expect our will to enjoy fulfillment with necessary regularity. It is also mistaken to chalk up the absence of answered prayer simply to deficient faith, as if we can, as a matter of fact, ultimately exert a determinative power over God through faith. In this view it is only the sinful person who is subordinate to God's reign; the person who pushes the right buttons elevates himself above it. This sinister view distorts prayer into a magic spell.

In the denial of what we petition we experience that God stands over us and is greater than our thinking and willing. But that does not jeopardize the complete integrity of the promise to answer prayer, since that promise would be invalid only if our prayers found a lesser kindness in God than we had given him credit for. What we find, however, is always the opposite, even when our request goes unmet: God exceeds what we presumed, with grace vaster and richer than we expected. Whoever experiences this is strengthened, not weakened, through the denial of requests made in prayer.[3]

---

3. When Paul (2 Cor. 12:7–9) is not hindered by the denial of his prayer request, but is rather fortified in prayer, then his conduct is on eminently firm logical and ethical grounds, since the denial of a petition is based on the truth that "the grace of Christ suffices for him." The oft-heard claim that absence of response to prayer amounts to

The promise given to prayer demonstrates its truth continually through uniting us with God. In so doing it always imparts to us the highest good, a good that far transcends whatever value might have inhered in the concrete content of our prayers. This by no means supports the view that all prayer may seek to do, or has the ability to do, is affect religious mood. This would again be to trivialize human initiative to the point of the annihilation of the will, and it would bifurcate our inner life by separating our religiously tinged feeling from the actual course of our life. The most important calling assigned to us, however, is the one that makes us partake of God. When this takes place, we have been graced with the most substantial and effectual experience conceivable. Nothing is greater, nothing mightier, than our person-to-person bond with God.

Since answers to prayer come about through natural agencies, the fruits of prayer for our lives both inwardly and outwardly are not to be regarded as some special domain apart from the entire course of daily occurrence. Yet prayer remains one of the most important means of conviction for the rise and maintenance of the certainty of God. Prayer often springs forth from persons in the most natural manner, and they know that to call on God is not delusion but highest truth and reason.[4] In these spontaneous acts of prayer we find that faith does not indwell us because of ingenuity and coercion; rather, we really do possess an internal openness for God and can be claimed by him. Every granted prayer confirms this clearly, whether the answer comes through an ostensibly predictable and visible causal chain or whether it surprises us with its improbability. Every supplicant receives enough granted petitions that the impulse to pray is sustained in him and does not die off for lack of results.

Prayer is always an act that unites us since it does not tolerate being restricted to our individual experiences. The egotist or individualist has already by definition forsaken veneration of God, but such a person will also forsake his thanking and requesting if he limits the scope of his gratitude and desire to his own receiving and use. Egotists become mute before

---

an objection against prayer, or presents a difficulty to praying, takes the same wrong turn as the skeptic who because of the failure of his thinking vilifies all thinking, or the mystic who because of the abominable nature of his desires does away with the will. The manner in which we functioned in prayer was misguided; the problem did not lie in prayer itself. Absence of response to prayer serves to adjust a particular concrete prayer request, but it is not a compelling argument against prayer.

4. A historically significant example: Bismarck's first prayer after a long stretch of prayerlessness (first letter among the letters to his wife). The example is all the more instructive because this prayer was not granted, yet marks the turn in his inner history. The welling up of prayer, not the granting of prayer, is experienced as the demonstration of the divine grace, for this reason: In prayer man becomes conscious that he is able to exercise faith. Because faith has been given to him, he knows that he has experienced God's grace.

Appendix B

God.[5] Both the things that are given to us and the achievements that we must actively perform extend far beyond the individual life, so that in giving thanks we recall not only what we have received but also the giftedness of others. Likewise, in supplication we bring not only our need but that of the other person before God. For prayer to be true and eligible for God to grant, it is essential that we be prayerfully conscious that God's relationship with us at the same time embraces all. Because prayer always becomes gratitude for the gift and strength of the other person, too, not just ourselves, and because petition arises for the need and tasks of others, not just us, prayer must be a corporate and not merely private act. Fellowship is perfected when we become one before God in petition, in thanks, and in worship. We possess a complete fellowship to the extent that our fellowship includes common prayer. A family is really and fully interconnected to the extent that it can draw together in prayer. We can talk of church to the extent that the fellowship of prayer reaches—and only to that extent. Christendom comprises the number of those who pray the Lord's Prayer in such a way that Jesus' prayer is their will. But if common prayer is to be possible, we have to heed fully Jesus' warning of the ruinous effect of publicity on prayer (Matt. 6:5–6). Prayer comes about only when we turn to God with decisive withdrawal from all that people mean for us. For this the secrecy of prayer is an absolute necessity. But the disappearance of the world and people does not have the effect of making their welfare and ruin of no matter to us. Prayer in the "prayer closet," too, is prayer for others, and thus an act that unites us with them. Now, when regard for man is banned from the center of our praying, we become capable of collective prayer that is really prayer and that appeals to God. The strengthened possibility of collective prayer being granted is given with the fact that the aim of divine grace is not fulfilled in the individual alone; rather, it first comes to full expression in the larger group of those bound together into a communion. God grants his reign not merely to isolated individual lives but to the church. That is why the church's prayer, too, is mighty in his presence. At the same time the fellowship of prayer confers ethical integrity on what we pray.

Persistence in prayer is vital because it leads us to communion with God. The goal to "pray without ceasing" (1 Th. 5:17) cannot, however, be attained by breaking off connection with the world and withdrawing from work for the sake of the world. That would be the surest way to silence our

---

5. Regarding the fact that the Enlightenment seriously damaged not only Catholic but also Protestant prayer, cf. e.g. Kant's opinion of prayer. Notice that in Protestant orthodoxy the believer was occupied only with his own blessedness, without relating it actively to the work of the congregation. If we had nothing to desire than that we remain in the faith until we finally die having preserved our blessed state, our prayer would of necessity flag. Nor can prayer receive sufficient basis and substance when our religious mandate is reduced solely to our natural occupation and natural suffer-

prayers, for without our work prayer lacks impetus and substance. Our will remains active only through the exercise of what we are called to do, and only in doing it do we receive limitless raw material to sustain prayer. It is our task to preserve simultaneously a connection in two directions, to God and to man, without the one activity hampering the other. The fact that in concrete life we are often conscious of only one or the other of these connections is unavoidable and normal. Still, the persistence of faith brings with it a persistent interaction with God that permeates our entire life.

We can therefore find the Christ only in that one who, through his name, grants us the right to pray and provides guidelines for its exercise.

Appendix C

Adolf Schlatter on Method in New Testament Theology

Discussions about the academic discipline of theology have often been rather feeble. This is because scholars have simply described the aim of their own work and suggested that that is the whole of the intellectual task with which the subject matter confronts us. This sort of illusion was encouraged by the fashion for making elaborate constructions that the dominance of speculative aims brought into the theology of the nineteenth century. It is probably safe to say that since then we have learned that none of us can write "the" definitive New Testament theology. But the clarification of the relationship of one's own aims to the intellectual task as a whole *is* justified when we are consciously making use of the available methods and systematizing what we observe. Anyone who has read my *Theology of the*

This essay originally appeared as "The Theology of the New Testament and Dogmatics," in Robert Morgan, ed., *The Nature of New Testament Theology*, Studies in Biblical Theology, 2nd series, no. 25 (London: SCM Press, 1973), pp. 117–66. Used by permission of SCM Press.

Appendix C

New Testament will perhaps understand why I wish to formulate the principles that have directed my work.

The Objection to a Historical Theology of the New Testament

Anyone who claims that New Testament theology is a historical discipline, that branch of historical research which sets out the convictions expressed in the writings of the New Testament and investigates their origin, is faced with a strong objection to his project. He will be told that he is aiming for the impossible; to make New Testament theology independent of dogmatics is an illusory fiction.

This skeptical view is widespread because it can be held from utterly opposing dogmatic positions. It alternates between being used as an attack on Christianity and as a defense of it. When it is linked with a powerful Christian dogmatics it can even become an accusation that the allegedly "historical" treatment of the Word of the New Testament is a serious misfortune for our peoples and churches. This is because it is supposed to corrupt theological work at its very roots and dangerously to injure the faith of the man in the pew.

To deal with this skeptical view, it is necessary to be clear about the difference between dogmatics and historical work. Our work has a historical purpose when it is not concerned with the interests that emerge from the course of our own life, but directs its attention quite deliberately away from ourselves and our own contemporary interests, back to the past. Our own convictions, which determine our thought and will, are held at a distance. We keep them out of the investigation so that we can see the subject matter as it was. Its effect on us and the way in which it might tie in with our own thinking and willing is not at this point brought into the field of our observation.

As historians, therefore, we can give only a partial answer to the overall question of truth. Our judgments about what was the case are subject to its norms without reserve. However, in historical work we do not allow the question of truth to go further than this. The question about what these ideas mean for us—whether and how they may be true for us also—does not belong here. Our goal is reached when we know what was once true for others. Yet since we cannot pose the question of truth simply in this limited way, there is always bound to be a further task alongside the historical one. That is the dogmatic task, which goes on to ask questions about the truth of what is said in the unlimited sense of how it determines our own thinking and willing. We are confronted not only with the past but also with the present, not only with what once happened inside other people but also with what is happening inside ourselves. The past sets us the question of what those who were there experienced at that time. Similarly, our present experiences confront us with the question of the content of our own thinking and willing.

When the dogmatician understands the question of truth to be what determines his own thinking—when he tries to perceive and express what was not only a reality and truth for others, but is also true for himself—he does not abandon history. He does not make himself into a hermit who withdraws from the community that gives foundation and content to all our thinking. Rather, he establishes this community more effectively and completely than the historian can. It is, of course, a common misunderstanding that, since the dogmatician orders his own relationship to his subject matter, he describes nothing but his own self-consciousness. It has been thought that he makes judgments that are valid for himself alone and proclaims his own experiences. German dogmaticians since Schleiermacher have often lent support to this misunderstanding by the remarkable way in which they have worn their convictions on their sleeves. However, dogmatic work demands of our observation and judgment the strictest objectivity. It demands this no less than historical work, because we only get any content for our own lives through bringing ourselves in our perceiving and willing into contact with what has happened.

What happens inside ourselves is dependent upon what is going on around us; our present experiences are dependent upon other people's past experiences. If our knowledge and will were applied simply to ourselves, they would perish. The direction and success of our own lives are measured by the power and fullness of the reality with which we make contact. So the dogmatician is also constantly concerned with history, not only with his own history that he cannot separate from that of others, but also with the history that has happened and is happening outside himself. If he were to abandon the material of history he would become a dreamer. This is true not only of Christian dogmatics but of every conviction. A person can only become clear about the course of his own life by seeing the past as it exercises its power upon us. And only thus can he cast any light upon what it is that creates a unity out of many individual lives. But even then, when he studies history, the dogmatician allows the question of truth its full significance—a significance that encroaches upon us, too. He continues to stand in the present situation, in which and for the sake of which he is engaged in thought. The past is important for him as an effective reality in his own experience.

It is impossible to use the term "dogma" to mark off the two areas from each other, even though the word is used to describe one branch of theology. When we call the theological activity that describes God's relation to us as it determines us "dogmatics," we are using the word with respect to that *shared* knowledge and faith that unites us into a church. We are saying that this reference of dogmatics to a shared knowledge and faith is an essential characteristic of it, and is what gives it its importance. The conviction of an individual is not automatically "dogma." It only becomes dogma when it is the common property of a group that derives its unity from it.

The result of the New Testament proclamation was the church. It is united not in the first place on the basis of its cultic or ethical action, and not simply because its members have similar feelings. Its unity is based upon shared certainties, without which those other things cannot be achieved. For this reason the formation of dogma has always been a fact of church history, and will continue to be one for as long as there is a church. It will always be an important concern of Christianity to think out and make clear what ideas have the right and the power to unite us with one another. But it is not appropriate to invoke this task of the dogmatician for distinguishing his job from New Testament theology. This is because New Testament theology also directly affects our unity as a church. Its progress strengthens this unity and its neglect threatens and weakens it. It would be wrong to say that New Testament theology is the concern of scholars, whereas dogmatics is the concern of Christianity. The church did not emerge on the basis of the thoughts of its members—not even of its dogmaticians—but through the work of Jesus and his messengers. It remains alive by preserving its connection with this history. The fact that the New Testament history and the word that witnesses to it is the ground of Christianity's existence is expressed by the fact that the New Testament is its canon. For this reason, the work of trying to understand it touches upon what is central to Christianity and gives it its unity just as directly as does dogmatics. Its results become the common possession of all members of the group just as much as do those of dogmatics. Its errors are just as damaging to our common life as are the false tacks of the dogmatician. Since Christianity is based upon the New Testament, the interpretation of the New Testament is an act that touches its foundations.

The concept of system is an even less appropriate one to use to describe the difference between historical and dogmatic work. We aim at systematization because we desire unitariness and completeness in our thinking. As such, it guides historical work no less than dogmatics. Our knowledge of history is not limited to scattered and contradictory observations. Here, too, the harmonious ordering of our thoughts is an indication that our work has been successful.

If, of course, by system one means the sort of thinking associated with phrases like "pure reason" and a priori, then it must be rigorously distinguished from historical work. The latter rests entirely on observation and demands wide-open eyes and the sort of whole-hearted surrender that perceives that with which it is presented. But in any case, if the notion of systematics is taken to imply that our thinking is independent of observation and can lead us to produce something out of ourselves, then it is of no more use to the dogmatician than to the historian. A dogmatician who no longer observes, but only forms judgments without first perceiving, and who instead of being given his ideas by reality, procures them for himself by free construction, is at best a poet and at worst a dreamer. Again, if we are to apprehend the factors leading to our existence, receiving takes precedence over construction. We cannot create anything without reference to what is given. However we set the question of truth, whether we direct it outwards toward what has happened before us, or inwards to what is happening within us, it is always related to something that is *given,* through which we are formed. Whatever we achieve by way of thinking remains connected throughout with what is already given for our work.

If by the idea of system we are considering the completeness of our knowing, it indicates a goal that far exceeds the limits of what we can do. But here, too, there is no difference between the two fields. The historian can never flatter himself that he has achieved a perfect knowledge of a matter. Rather, with his observing and understanding he is for ever standing before limits that he cannot remove, since his knowledge inevitably ends where the testimony of his sources ends. Our knowledge of what is past rests on memory. But wherever there is memory there is also forgetting. Forgetting is just as indispensable for our intellectual life as memory is. If there were no forgetting, the difference between past and present would disappear. Precisely because what is past and gone is always partly forgotten, history will never be a fully completed science.

But the goal of perfect knowledge is just as unattainable for the dogmatician as it is for the historian. We can no more penetrate our own existence with an all-embracing knowledge than we can the past. In dogmatics also, we are dependent upon what individual certainties we can attain without being able to make them up into a perfect whole. For this reason the first and most important aim of both types of work is not to be found in what is meant by the word "system." It is, rather, that our thinking should be true to its own norms. Our first duty as historians or dogmaticians is to shield our thinking from inappropriate assumptions. Our thinking has had an indestructible value when it has been obedient to the norm of truth, even if it has been unable to achieve systematic completion in all sorts of ways. If the will that guides our thinking immediately strays away from obedience to the norms of thought toward the perfection of a system, then both historical and dogmatic work equally degenerate into a fabrication of conjectures, and become an intellectual game.

What is the basis for the widespread skepticism about the correctness of this division of the theological field? It appeals to the character of the New Testament word, which confronts us with the claim that we should be affected by it in all our behavior and without reserve. For this reason the dogmatic question may not be set aside in favor of merely historical investigation. According to the skeptical position, it is true that the historian explains; he observes the New Testament neutrally. But in reality this is to begin at once with a determined struggle against it. The word with which the New Testament confronts us intends to be believed, and so rules out once and for all any sort of neutral treatment. As soon as the historian sets aside or brackets the question of faith, he is making his concern with the New Testament and his presentation of it into a radical and total polemic against it.

The attitude of historians and the course of historical research strengthen this skepticism. It is argued that the historian has never in fact succeeded in doing what the New Testament denies to be permissible, and in its own way makes impossible. If he claims to be an observer, concerned solely with his object, then he is concealing what is really happening. As a matter of fact, he is always in possession of certain convictions, and these determine him not simply in the sense that his judgments derive from them, but also in that his perception and observation are molded by them.

It is clear that without the honest attempt to lay aside all personal concerns and the opinions of one's school or party, and seriously to *see*, academic work degenerates into hypocrisy. But even this honest attempt cannot overcome the fact that an observer sees with his own eyes only what the certainties that internally determine him allow him to perceive. The argument runs as follows.

All this should be evident from the course of church history. New Testament theology as an independent subject only dates from the Enlightenment. Up to that point the church had no need of it, even though from the beginnings its desire for Christian knowledge operated in an environment characterized by strong intellectual tensions. What was looked for here was supplied by dogmatics alone, and in such a way that nothing beyond it was needed. The Enlightenment, on the other hand, fought for the distinction between the two areas because it was guided by a polemical tendency that was working for emancipation from the tradition of the church. Since this was supported and sanctified by the New Testament, it was natural for there to be a desire to remove the New Testament to a distance from the observer where it became nothing but the object of historical consideration. Then the difference between the New Testament and the church's teaching would become clear, and both could be robbed of their power by being played off against each other.

The history of the discipline of New Testament theology then confirms this in that the variations that mark its new epochs are always occasioned by outside influences. They are not brought about by its own work but by the dogmatic convictions which, independent of this, have gained power in our academic life. In the work of the rationalists, Jesus and his messengers themselves looked like rationalists. Then this type of New Testament theology disappeared, not because of historical work but because of speculative Kantianism. Here the work of New Testament theology divided into different schools, and alongside the Schleiermacherian type there appeared the Hegelian. Again a change was then stimulated by influences lying outside purely historical work; namely, as historical research was accommodated to the methods of the natural sciences, and all religious criteria were excluded from the historical approach. If the work of New Testament theology joins in all those debates evoked by argument about these convictions that are fundamental for our consciousness of ourselves and of God,[1] then its historical objectivity is illusory.

The consequence has been that those presentations of New Testament ideas that antedate the discipline of New Testament theology, such as for example Calvin's *Institutes*, have incomparably greater scientific value even as history than much of what has been done with all the tools of modern historical technique. The reason for this is not the intellectual weakness of the historians, but lies in their methods. The older writers were most seriously attentive to the relationship between what the New Testament said and the convictions by which they themselves were determined. They were therefore resolved to clarify its contents and be certain about its truth-value. The modern historian, on the other hand, lays the ideas that determine him on one side, saying that they are his own business and not affected by his science. In fact, however, they do inevitably exercise an influence, though this is now concealed by the fiction of a merely historical purpose. They are therefore untested and ungrounded, and often enough even the historian himself is unconscious of them. With the same facility with which he passes lightly over his own convictions, he now makes judgments on the apostolic statements, too. How he interprets them and evaluates them is, of course, irrelevant for his own thought. He operates merely "historically," merely upon an object that is dead and gone.

The result of this is the present situation that we can all see. The struggle for and against Christianity no longer takes place alone or in the main through dogmatic work, but predominantly in the field of historical research, particularly in New Testament theology. Historical investigations serve as weapons for the attack and defense of religious positions. It is therefore clear that the historian's objectivity is self-deception, and that the convictions that influence him have a dominating influence upon his work. Otherwise why would there be this struggle? Polemic is not a feature of historical work, but grows out of dogmatics. So the fact that historical literature is put at the disposal of religious polemic as much as it evidently is, means that it has formally and openly contradicted the independence of

---

1. Schweitzer's review of the "historical" treatment of the life of Jesus contains a number of solid observations on this point.

historical research. So the earlier position of theology, in which history and dogmatics were intertwined, has been reestablished. A psychologically well-grounded law has operated here, one that removes the artificial distinctions made by the teaching work of the theological faculties. In an age when Nietzsche's *Antichrist* and Harnack's *What Is Christianity?* are widely read books, it is a singular archaism to speak of historical work on the New Testament, work that is only concerned to perceive what has happened. This archaism can only be explained as a result of the isolation of academics, which is comparable to that of a painter who is decorating the walls of a house with frescoes while flames burst out of the roof.

The Obligation to Historical Work

If the allocation of New Testament theology to the realm of history implied a rupture of its connection with dogmatics, then it really would be nothing but a fiction that ought to disappear. The skeptical view as sketched out above is correct in saying that to label this task historical can never mean that the convictions that determine us no longer affect us when we are performing it. No improvement in the art of writing history could achieve this, and it should not try to, because a discipline that would make us into a lifeless mirror for the past would be an inhuman undertaking. It cannot be done, and so its results are worthless. At no point in our lives do we have the task of self-annihilation. That remains true even when the demand for this self-annihilation is qualified by its being limited to the moment of doing a particular job.

All efforts at self-annihilation only result in the disturbance of our own human existence. Our being confronted by the past, and its demand to be seen as it was, does not mean that we should annihilate the present. It is true that when other people are the object of our perception and understanding we are required in some way to get free from our own selves. This leads to a genuine surrender of ourselves to other people, and indeed only a person who is prepared to give himself in this way can receive. But this conscious turning away from our own selves is never self-annihilation. Someone who wanted to deny and destroy himself in this surrender would not have given anything.

Making a man into a machine for observing is nowhere less feasible than with regard to the New Testament; because, regardless of whether a person appropriates its content or keeps it at a distance, still his will is involved at the deepest level. So in every piece of work done according to the norms of historical science, the writer and the reader should be aware that a historical sketch can only take shape in the mind of a historian, and that in this process the historian himself, with all his intellectual furniture, is involved. If this fact is lost sight of, then it is no longer science in which we are involved, but crazy illusions.

The connection between historical science and dogmatics, between the experience of others and that of oneself, between the history that happened once and the history that is happening now, cannot be set aside until historical work is complete—as though only its completed results are instructive for the dogmatician, and determine his judgments. That would be to perceive only a half of what is going on here. The relationship between the two functions is there right from the beginning of historical work, and it is a matter of interreaction. It does not simply come in at the end, but permeates the whole course of historical work.

The dogmatician in us supplies the historian with the capacity for making judgments through which he distinguishes between what is possible and what is not, and between what in the outline of history produces effects and what is dead. When we look at the past, our knowledge of the present enables us to clarify what happened and the forces that gave it shape. The relation between the two functions that we are discussing will never be established in terms of merely one-sided dependence, as though one had exclusive priority and so was the cause and giver, whereas the other was exclusively secondary, on the receiving end and getting its shape from the first. In fact, in the unity of human existence there is always a two-way connection between them both. Both are involved in giving and receiving.

The relation between historical research and dogmatics leaves no room for the question which is in control and which is derivative. Neither is simply independent; neither is merely the basis of the other. And neither is merely derivative or conditioned. Historical research has its independent foundation in the completeness of the past. Similarly, the certainty of dogmatics is something *primary* that influences all our looking back to what has happened, because it arises out of the present and apprehends what is creative of our own human existence.

The historian's neutrality becomes a fiction when it leads to insistence on a complete separation between these two distinct functions. At the present time, the historical literature on the New Testament is overladen with conjectures that are offered to us as history. The reasons for this are partly our failure to *observe,* and the appearance of imagination in place of observation. But also there is the failure of historians to give some account of the motives that determine them. They assume that their "presuppositionless history" gives them the power to overlook and not subject to criticism the presuppositions that do in fact determine them. However, we shall in fact only get free of and rise above our presuppositions by paying conscious and rigorous attention to them.

All this does not mean that the separate development of our two functions is contradicted or shown to be impossible. We are not talking here

Appendix C

about a carving up of the self into two centers of thought that exist in isolation. We are talking rather of two *functions*. They do possess in the unity of human existence something that always holds them together. But a certain independence is also called for, corresponding to the variety of responses that enrich our existence.

What has happened in the past demands of us, by the very fact that it *has* happened, that we grasp it in its *givenness*. The question here is whether we are all wrapped up in ourselves, or whether we are able to be genuinely open to the past so as to be able to see things other than ourselves. I believe that we are given a capacity for seeing. But this cannot be proved to someone who denies it. The rule "Do and you will know" applies here. As is the case with all fundamental convictions, *action* is the potency that shapes our consciousness.

Now if our viewing is to cut loose from ourselves and be free to grasp what is there to see, then the process will have to be neat and complete, and this is assisted by a distinction between historical work and the dogmatic question. If we turn our attention straight away to the connections that exist between our object and our own ideas and will, then there is always a danger that we will break off our observation at the point where our own interest in the object ends. Our perception might be directed exclusively toward what we can at once make our own.

Church history gives an urgent reminder of our duty to use our eyes steadfastly and with no other motive than to perceive the object. When the Enlightenment, polemically motivated as it was, demanded a biblical dogmatics in place of the church's tradition, and so brought about the birth of New Testament theology, it had a very good case. This was because the church's capacity for observation had in fact been seriously damaged by a confusion of the two tasks. The church's judgments about the relationship between Scripture and church doctrine and action, between the faith of the New Testament and its own piety, were often very confused. Different lines that sometimes even crossed each other were often bundled together, and this lack of clarity had equally damaging effects upon the historical and the dogmatic sides. However, clarity about the relationship of the church's action to the word of Scripture is advanced when in the first place the question of the content of the New Testament statements is resolutely put for its own sake, and when we have an intellectual discipline whose only concern is to know and to understand what is *there* in the New Testament.

The justification for a New Testament theology conceived as history is that the independent development of historical science gives a measure of protection, admittedly not infallible, against arbitrary reconstructions of its object. It secures us against producing a mixture of what Scripture says and what the church teaches, or a mixture of the Bible and our own religious opinions, in which neither the one factor nor the other is correctly grasped and fruitfully applied. The historian's good conscience consists in his being clear about what he believes and why. Conversely, the good conscience of the Christian dogmatician, and his ability to mediate effectively what the New Testament presents us with both to himself and the church, is partly dependent upon the faithfulness and success with which we do our historical work on the New Testament.

If the objector says that this historical work is no longer opportune today, the history of modern thought can be used to contradict him. It is clear from the literature on New Testament theology as well as from other fields how modern thinking is opposed to the older logical ideal. Formerly the dominant concerns of thought were taken from "reason" and its concepts, and the intention was to form ideas that were universally valid. Now, however, people are concerned even in their thinking to do justice to the personal life of the individual. The justification for an idea is no longer based on its origin in and contribution to a common stock of ideas, but rather on its derivation from personal experience and expression of that in all its concrete particularity.

So if a person brings his own individual concerns and his own personal experience to the New Testament history in order to confirm the legitimacy of his relationship to it, his observation in this particular direction will be considerably sharpened. But at the same time, this association of the past with the particular act of one's will that guides one's observation in the present, is very dangerous. In the modern period, when our thinking is more individualistic than formerly, it is particularly important that we cultivate those historical concerns that require of us the selfless act of genuine seeing. Through this act, our heightened individual life is augmented by coming into a full, effective relationship with the reality outside and above itself. Our thinking and willing thus become a part of the wider human community.

Reflections based on the laws that govern our thinking activity do not conflict with the claim that the apostolic word makes upon us. They are, rather, confirmed by it, since the demand for faith requires the clarity of an observation that is selfless and complete. No doubt this claim does contain the summons to a union that submits us to it complete with all that we are. That does not mean, however, that we can tailor it according to our requirements. It does not stand there like a beggar asking for a gift—the gift of understanding, acknowledgment and practical application. Since its purpose is to provide a foundation for our faith, it stands above us and forbids us to mix it up with the substance of our own mind. We are not to cut it down to the size of our own thinking and willing. The demand for faith contains within itself a claim to sovereignty. This claim comes from God's goodness and so does not aim to humiliate and impoverish us, but to grant us life and gifts. However, for the same reason, it never ceases to demand

Appendix C

a resolute and complete subordination of ourselves to it. The New Testament makes this claim because of what it is in itself. It can only be allowed this claim if it can give grounds for it by its own contents. For this reason it must be perceived as it actually is.

It is, of course, true that the historian's position of neutrality vis-à-vis the word of Jesus cannot be his last act, nor can it regulate his relationship to that word. The word does not let hovering on the fence go on indefinitely. What the end-result of a historian's work means for the historian depends upon the history that takes place inside him. This is given him by a kind of dogma that shapes his own experience.

The Limits of New Testament Theology

Doubts about the correct purpose to be assigned to New Testament theology can also take the form of wanting to make it into the theologian's sole and final task. It is said that the sequence of ideas with which the New Testament confronts us does demand to be examined historically, but that when this is done the work of theology is finished. There is no room for a second discipline alongside this one, which would exist as a strange sort of parallel to it. When New Testament theology has done its job successfully, according to this view, Christianity is understood and a judgment on it achieved.

This line of argument is also to be found linked with opposing religious standpoints. It may take the following form. When the New Testament is fitted into the course of the history that produced it, its claim upon us is done for and the Christ sinks into the past. Or it may be argued that when a New Testament statement is given to our understanding, what is given is the ground of our faith. The only other processes of mediation that are necessary for us, if the New Testament witness is to stir us, belong simply to the sphere of the will. It is now a matter of obedience. Therefore anything beyond New Testament theology is the concern of life, not of academic work.

Both of these standpoints might concede that there may be intellectual obstacles that get in the way of a correct attitude to the New Testament. These can be investigated by the science that is concerned with pathological processes. One side will call in Enlightenment man to remove religious prejudices. The other side will call in the religious apologist who is concerned with those conditions of the consciousness that are responsible for the denial of God and the repudiation of Christ, and will try to overcome such disturbances. But dogmatics has always been definitely distinct from apologetics, because its work is not in the first place directed toward cases of degeneration or confusion in the consciousness; rather, it strives to achieve the sort of knowledge that gives a positive basis to the faith of the community and the individual. It is being said here, however, that this goal is reached with New Testament theology.

These are some of the reasons why in pre-Reformation and Reformation theology there was never any distinction between the theology of the New Testament and that of the church. A unitary system of doctrine, like for example Calvin's *Institutes*, was the only legitimate form of doctrine. It seemed to be a consequence of the basic idea of the gospel that once established, a scriptural statement should get itself across into our thinking and willing under its own power. There should be no further need of mediation.

Nevertheless, the church has never limited its intellectual activity simply to hearing the New Testament. Its thought has always traveled in different directions, beyond what is given us in the New Testament. This should not be judged a fault nor considered as degeneration. It arises directly out of the relationship in which the New Testament stands to us. So it crops up, though in a variety of modifications and individual forms, whenever and wherever the New Testament is operating.

Since the attitude to which the New Testament calls us and leads us is faith, our agreeing with it follows through our own personal act. This, however, means that the New Testament statement and the content of our own consciousness should enter into discussion and mutually come to terms. Only this can ensure that our acknowledgment of the apostolic word takes place without an inner break: not by violence or coercion, but with a willing and whole-hearted openness of ourselves for it. Only this can plant it in our personal existence.

To elevate the New Testament theology in itself to the status of dogmatics would be to work with an un-Christian conception of obedience and to try to subject ourselves to it in such a way that we no longer remain in possession of what we are. This is a self-contradiction that always fails. It leads to the well-known hybrid, disobedient obedience, which we have seen often enough in the history of the church.

If the presentation of the New Testament statements needed nothing more than an order to us to conserve what was already known, then our going along with it would become an achievement of our will. That, however, is something different from the sort of faith the New Testament asks of us. The New Testament calls for certainty. It is also a matter of choice— but not a choice which lacks any basis. This choice knows what it is choosing and why it is choosing it. Its grounds cannot be established without thought. So Christianity has always recognized that the New Testament confronts it with a double question. There is not only the question of what the New Testament itself presents to be heard and understood by us, but also the question directed toward us: how that message is related to the content of our own intellectual being.

Appendix C

These far-reaching tasks do not arise only as a result of intellectual degeneration, though this may unfortunately gain ground as much in the intellectual climate of nations as in the consciousness of individuals. But our task is not simply that of bringing health by the removal of illusions and the clearing away of such forms of the will as have to be rejected. It is also the case that we bring to the New Testament something of value, and the relation of this to the New Testament has to be determined.

In the first place we bring those thoughts that stem from human nature. But that is not all—as though our sole task were to unite our natural consciousness with the consciousness of God given us by Jesus. We also bring religious values. This is partly because our communion with God does not come to us only as something extra and from outside, but gives us our existence and essence. It is also because the church, through which the content of the intellect is given us, and the course of our lives, which shapes us inwardly, are both themselves tools that serve God's sovereignty and his grace. They do not simply obstruct and obscure our thinking and willing. They also fill them with God's good gifts. Our relationship to the New Testament is one of subordination. It is not described correctly when an absolute contrast is made between the present as utterly deserted by God and untouched by his rule, and a past that was filled with the revelation of God. This not only contradicts our experience, which is forever mediated to us by our own life and that of our church, but also contradicts what the apostles say. They do not see the conclusion of Jesus' work being followed by the night of total abandonment by God. There remains an indestructible reconciliation that summons the world to God. There remains Christ's rule that spans the aeons, and there remains the presence of the Spirit that leads the believer's knowing and willing from God to God. This is the indestructible basis of the fact that the word of Scripture stands over the church, and a clear indication of that fact. It also makes it impossible for the church ever to be content to be nothing but a receptacle for the word of Scripture, and merely a repetition or imitation of the first disciples. It has its own independent life, and that life is something of value.

New Testament theology itself sharpens our eyes for this independent life of the church by showing how primitive Christianity's expression of its faith was rooted in its own historical situation, and is therefore something individual and unrepeatable. By confronting us with the peculiar life of the apostolic community and clarifying it for us, New Testament theology makes it impossible for us to transform the New Testament into a series of abstract statements and models that hover around suspended over and above reality. It also strengthens our awareness of the need for dogmatic work, because when we are thus aware that what was once the case can only become real in a particular moment of the past course of history, then the question cannot be avoided: How is what once happened in the past

182

made new in the present? How can we verify that something is the cause of our own being alive when it came into existence in a life that has in part become foreign to us?

For this reason the religious question is never settled by simply handing on what Scripture says. The question is always: What does Scripture mean *for us?* This "us," with all it involves, takes us into the realm of dogmatics, and the dogmatician does not fulfil his task simply by becoming a New Testament theologian. He has to give concrete and tangible content to the picture of that humanity to which he himself belongs and for which he does his work. It is for this generation of humanity that he works at a form of dogma that is not simply imposed on us from outside, but arises naturally from within, and so can become a bond uniting the community.

The same considerations apply to those who tell us that once they have a historical account of the New Testament they can get free of its claim upon them. They, too, can only bypass the act of thinking because they have already made up their minds about the question of God and the will. If they cannot give good grounds for their decision, then as well as showing the fettered dependence of those religious people who will not think, they also evidence that self-glorying arbitrariness that undertakes to determine our relationship to the world by its own power. Both these ways of destroying our will are similar, and are causally related to each other. If, on the other hand, their will knows what it is denying and why it is repudiating the Word of Jesus, then they, too, are basing their relationship to the New Testament on dogmatic work. Their dogma is different from the one the Christian dogmatician gets from the New Testament and has as his conviction only in its result. Its object and purpose are the same.

The uncertainty that is obvious in current work on New Testament theology is partly connected with the question of the relation between historical work and dogmatics. If we are controlled by the idea that what we perceive in the New Testament is meant to become our own personal possession, then there is always the danger that historical work will be destroyed because the concrete individuality of what happened is replaced by ideal pictures—pictures that are supposed to show the meaning of assurance of God, communion with Christ, love, faith and repentance, to the piety of every age. This tendency is strengthened by the seductive glitter that our intellectual activity gives to abstractions. It can often appear as though abstractions are the surest means of getting the New Testament statements to take effect in our own thinking, because of the way they float indefinitely in the air. Does not the general embrace all particulars? Will not, therefore, "the permanent element in Christianity" consist in the ideal element? When Jesus is made into an "ideal man," and New Testament faith and love into an indefinite ideal picture of some sort of confidence and goodness, then their value seems secured for everyone. The concrete individualized character of a real event, on the other hand, makes it unrepeatable, and to some extent even incomprehensible.

However, when we no longer see in the New Testament what the piety of the early period was, but only what ought to be the Christianity of every age, the historian is no longer giving the dogmatician what he ought to be giving him, because the historical task is obscured. The dogmatician also needs realities. He cannot be satisfied with the supposed nature of faith, but must know how God created faith. An idea of what the church ought to be is not enough. He needs to perceive *that* a community emerged whose peculiar characteristic was its relation to God, and *how* this community emerged. The relevant factor for him is not an image of Christ that merely gives expression to our own wishes, but a knowledge of what the Christ was like. Abstractions cut loose from realities are just as useless in practice as they are vacuous in theory.

Our task is to attach our concrete, historically conditioned lives to God. We get the necessary assurances for this not by logical fictions and ideas, but through facts. These facts do not come from ideal men, but from men like ourselves, and that means historically localized men who lived their lives with God as their source and their goal. Dogmaticians do not need a general conception of faith and love. What they need is a definite perception of what is meant by good will and confidence in God in the concrete situations of a human life.

This means that New Testament theology is not giving the dogmatician the material that he needs when it removes the temporal and spatial coloring from the New Testament events. It gives him what he needs by making the New Testament as accessible as our capacity for seeing allows. The task this gives to the dogmatician is then a large one, because he has to tie up the completed realities of the New Testament with the equally concrete and definite reality of his own life. But since this task is posed by the very fact of our human existence, it must not be broken off uncompleted.

In order to oppose the idealizing tendency that turns the New Testament statements into pallid abstractions, the current literature often shows a taste for giving the New Testament conceptions a touch of antiquity by fanciful turns of phrase. Since the texts themselves give no occasion for this, people bring in the supposed background to the material for the purpose. Jesus' words about God's royal sovereignty are thought to be the product of fiery apocalyptic dreams, and Paul's worship of Jesus is thought to be based on gnostic speculation about a preexistent primal man. Paul's distinction between the spirit and the flesh in himself and everyone else is supposed to derive from his view of everything being penetrated by an ethereal fluid that he called the Holy Spirit, and so on. The scent of antiquity on the apostolic word, which shows it to belong to the past, is made clear by a characteristic that is still incomprehensible to us. But the effort to shield the New Testament word from being accommodated to our own spiritual life goes wrong when it distracts historical work from the given material of the apostolic word itself. If we surround it with pieces of background that contradict its clear statements, we are making historical research into a work of fiction. In my view, New Testament theology only fulfils its obligations by observation, not by free creation.

Statistics and Etiology

The first task of New Testament theology consists in perceiving the given facts of the case, and it would be childish to worry that there is no more work left for us to do since countless scholars have been observing the New Testament for a long time now. That would show how little we were aware of the size of the task posed by the formula "observation." What has happened in the past far exceeds in its fullness and depth our capacity for seeing, and there is no question of an end being reached even of the first and most simple function of New Testament study; namely, seeing what is there.

But the task cannot be limited simply to this. It also embraces the observation of those processes through which the New Testament convictions emerged. We have to grasp as best we can how this happened. This research on the causes will also stimulate, broaden, and verify the primary work of observation.

It is admittedly conceivable to set up New Testament theology as consisting simply of a statistical account of the ideas in the New Testament.[2] The teaching activity of the church has always done this statistical work, even before New Testament theology existed as an independent discipline. The vast literature of commentary material on the New Testament serves this task. A New Testament theology sketched out as statistics only differs from a commentary in form. What a commentary establishes according to the given structure of the texts, this sort of New Testament theology sets out by subject matter. It is structured by the similarities and differences to be found in the doctrinal content of the statements, thus removing the form given by the documents.

But the significance of New Testament theology today rests on the fact that it is not content simply to gather material like a statistician. It sees its main task in raising the question how the convictions found here in the New Testament arose. It is concerned not only to perceive but to explain, and it really grasps what is related by showing the conditions through which the latter emerged. These sorts of questions neither damage the historical purpose of the investigation nor trespass upon the dogmaticians' territory.

---

2. This is how Bernhard Weiss sees the task in his New Testament Theology.

Appendix C

The inquiry concerns what gave rise to the ideas of the New Testament, and that is not a part of our own existence, but took place in the consciousness of early Christianity, or at least affected it.

Statistical work itself always leads to etiological considerations about how the history arose, considerations that touch on the processes that gave rise to the content of the New Testament. That is because what we have here is not a number of separate statements that lie there unrelated. The New Testament relates them with a living bond as ground and consequence, as what conditions and what is conditioned. The idea of causation does not have to be brought into the New Testament from outside. It is already powerfully present, because the New Testament itself grounds and develops its results before our eyes. This would not be the case if its contents consisted of abstractions, "concepts" cut loose from history, or if it contained a doctrinal norm with fixed formulas that exercised authoritative control without reference to their basis, or if what we had were mysteries where no account of their basis and meaning is either wanted or able to be given. None of these possibilities describes what was the case with the founding of the church. The men who were responsible for assembling the church showed remarkable power in forging links. They let their thought be controlled by a will that would convince other people and so established their dogma. Since what we have in the New Testament is not something beyond time and history, but rather living and evolving processes, purely statistical work that does not show this aspect of New Testament thought remains incomplete and incorrect.

The first task here is to note the connections that link up the individual statements of the apostles and show how one comes out of another. The conditions of any thought are, first of all, those processes that accompany it in consciousness. The apostles' statements reveal an internal life, surprisingly alike in its firm, all-controlling unitariness and in its richness. It thus confronts us with a claim to be understood and makes this possible. An account of Paul is inadequate if it tells us what he thought about flesh, how he understood the death of Jesus, what he counts as faith and how he values it, but fails to show how these judgments are related. One depends on another. It is not there for its own sake, but on account of its proximity to something else. Its distinctive content comes from its proper place in the unity of the apostle's total consciousness. By clarifying these connections we understand Paul. In this way we explain how he came to say, "I am crucified with Jesus" and why he evaluates nobody "according to the flesh," and why he sees faith as his righteousness.

Someone who tells us that John contains teaching about the Logos and that he has a negative view of the world, that his ethics are concentrated in the idea of love, and that you can see how for him faith in Jesus means a person's entry into eternal life, is still not fulfilling the historical task that is set us. In history one thing is as it is because of something else. John's statements are understood by perceiving how one produces another and how all reveal the same unitary will.

In all these directions the historical task is inexhaustible. It is posed in the same way by the word of Jesus. His sovereign will, his divine sonship, his witness to God's sovereignty, his call to repentance, his willing the cross, his fellowship with the disciples—in short the whole sequence of his acts—are not just one item after another. We fail to do them justice if we simply note each one separately. His knowledge of himself as Lord of the community is grounded in his filial relationship to God, in his knowing himself empowered to call sinners, and in his authority to bear his cross. Jesus will be comprehensible to us in proportion as these connections are perceived. It is thus that we grasp why he spoke with Nicodemus in one way and not another, why his command to his disciples was as the Sermon on the Mount tells us, and why he used the name "king" as is witnessed by the report of the crucifixion.

But it is also the case that our inner life is causally connected with our external situation. It therefore becomes understandable to us when we spell that out, too. All observations that draw out the connection of the New Testament statements with the history of Christianity belong here. So does the relationship of the apostolic preaching to the ideas of its surrounding world. The New Testament itself confronts us with this aim because it keeps before our eyes the firm connections between its history and its teaching. It tells us that its ideas took shape not in isolation from the surrounding world nor simply in a struggle against it, but under the control of a will to win it, and to correspond to the spiritual need of the time in such a way that its word might be understood and appropriated. In this work of seeking acceptance, Christian preaching was motivated by a strong love, and expressly used and fostered connections with what mankind already possessed.

We would therefore miss an important aspect of New Testament teaching if we repudiated the question whether and how far Christian convictions can be seen to connect causally with the intellectual background of the age. If agreement in sequences of thought can be shown here, this tells us something about their derivation. They cannot have sprung to birth each time as something completely new. Rather, they are causally connected and represent a coherent and unitary process.

The border between observation and supposition fluctuates here. So a flood of hypotheses, and with them rationalism and controversy, ensues. This obliges us to tread carefully, but at the same time compels us not to neglect this part of the work. We have to show so far as possible what sober observation directed to the facts can understand about the processes in which the ideas of the New Testament emerged.

Appendix C

Different constructions of New Testament theology emerge, depending on what methods are used to explain what we have. As early as the eighteenth century, attention to the special character of each New Testament writer caused it to be noticed that they all expressed their own individual ideas. We therefore have the job of making clear the particular type of piety shown by each of these types of teaching. This method has lasting validity because the history that is our concern here is very largely the product of community leaders; these men had the power to make the rich life they led visible, and to insert it into the whole subsequent course of history as effective potency.

This procedure brings out an essential characteristic of the early history of Christianity. This is that it is based upon those processes that constitute the personal existence of the individual, and succeeds by using nothing except what regulates the inner attitude of a man toward God. The individual is placed in a communion with God that is appropriate to him. The community's leaders thus possessed in their thinking and willing something granted them, and show their independence with striking power.

An account of Jesus should not depict a mass movement in Palestinian Jewry, but *him*. Similarly, the Christian mission in the Greek-speaking world was not sustained by a group of Paul's disciples, but by Paul, complete with the firm convictions his own history had given him. For this reason biographical investigation of Paul is indispensable.

Again, carving up John into a Johannine school was a wrong-headed conjecture. Here, too, world-historical influence attaches to the unique content of a strong individual life. Part of the task of New Testament theology is, therefore, to show the community leaders' intellectual and volitional links with their history and the differences between them. Because of this, New Testament theology must be divided into as many theologies as there are New Testament authors.

However, if only these methods are used, the field of vision is narrowed and an essential part of the history is lost. The eighteenth century, which created these methods, had forgotten the meaning of community and the power of social life to set history in motion. Early Christianity did not consist simply in a few apostles each producing a store of religious ideas and powerfully combining them into the unity of a personal life. What emerged at that time was the community, and this united the individuals in the harmony of a shared faith and action.

We have in the New Testament the phenomenon of the construction of dogmas. But it is not a matter of the imposition of a doctrinal norm from outside; rather, certainties evolve and take root in everyone, producing fellowship. The authenticity of this construction of dogmas is proved by the way in which it created a common will that united the community's action. Given this, New Testament theology cannot simply pass on to the differences, where the personal gifts and characteristics of individuals can be seen. Even these do not arise in isolation from the community, but in working for it. The apostle is, of course, older than the community, since it was assembled by him. But for that very reason, all his thinking and willing is directed toward the community, and it is a misunderstanding to see him as a solitary thinker in isolation from his vocation and activity. This theology is aimed at the community and takes its shape from it. Church and New Testament belong to the same evolutionary process. New Testament theology, therefore, is faced simultaneously with two tasks. Each individual formation is worthy of special attention. At the same time, one must take care to observe that all these perfectly free and personally believing men still constituted a unity. Their fitting into a complete organism and sharing a common task led to the evolution of the community.

A further essential difference in the total historical picture depends on whether we see in the New Testament views that grew up together, or whether we put them in sequence, with each one evolving from another. New Testament theologies sketched out on the basis of Hegelian dogma owe part of their strong influence to the unitary way in which they regarded the whole of the New Testament material in the light of the idea of development. The thought of Jesus was allowed only the role of the first impulse, introducing the whole movement. The conclusion of the movement was supposed to be found in John, who was considered the highest manifestation to emerge from early Christian history—though only when his Jewishness had been removed. The transition was supposed to have been caused by Paul and the reshaping of Christian convictions that he brought about. This schematization made a strong impression upon many people's imagination, and is widely thought to be the result of scientific investigation.

With the Hegelian starting-point came a concentration of interest in the particularities and oppositions in the New Testament doctrinal constructions. Here in the movement of ideas, diverging into oppositions and continuing through struggle, were sought the moving forces of all history and those that produced Christianity. Since metaphysical presuppositions are here directly woven into the historical picture and give it a dogmatizing tendency, historical work inevitably began to lurch. The ideas that were imported to explain the New Testament history stood in sharp opposition to the way in which the men of the New Testament themselves thought. For them God was not an idea nor simply the giver of ideas. Nor did they see struggle as the basis of their action. It was inevitable that history should be given a new shape in the form demanded by the dogma of the narrator. It can now be taken as generally agreed that the question of development in New Testament history must be kept free of all pressure from metaphysical laws.

Appendix C

The work of Jesus is clearly distinct from that of his community. It is the most important causal factor leading to doctrinal formulation in the New Testament. How far what followed from him was a genuine development uniting what the community achieved, with its source in what Jesus gave it, is at present a hotly disputed question. Motives that are not only foreign to Jesus but that would destroy his thought are frequently read into the New Testament. He did not seek to bring men into contact with God through magic. The community, however, is supposed to have gone in for this sort of magical means of producing salvation. He himself did not understand his sonship in a gnostic way, nor the effect of the divine spirit in a fanatical way. The community is said immediately to have joined gnostic theories to the divine sonship and fanatical tendencies to the idea of the spirit. It is therefore a dominant question in New Testament theology today whether the religious history of the community can be understood as a development of what was created through Jesus, or whether we have here to draw upon outside forces to make the movement of history comprehensible.

The question has its own form with regard to each of the disciples known to us. There is a considerable distance separating I Peter from the Peter of the Synoptic Gospels. The same is true of the Johannine literature and John in the Synoptic Gospels. Is this a matter of development, or of constructions that cannot be harmonized and do not belong within the development of a single life-span? This question is also posed with alluring depth in Paul, on the one hand by the way in which Colossians describes the community's fellowship with Christ, and on the other by the Pastoral Epistles. These epistles make capable leadership, proving itself in activity, into the characteristic mark of anyone who wants to work in the community. Are such remarks the final, most mature conclusion to the thought and will found in the earlier epistles, or do we have here extraneous elements even in these documents authenticated by the name of Paul?

Within the church an epoch is clearly marked by the transition of Christianity to the Greeks and the emergence of Greek communities. How was the new form different from the older form of the church, and in what way was it united with it? How are we to conceive the relation of the Palestinian teachers, Matthew, James, John and Peter, to each other and to Paul? All these questions demand precise observation, and so resistance to the attractions of fixed metaphysical theories. Such theories give food for the imagination, but not genuine knowledge. There are two opposing conceptions here. One sees the New Testament types as independent forms that grew up simultaneously and that derive their unity from the fact that they belong to the same community, and exercise the same gift of Jesus. The other view tries to derive one type from the other through direct dependence, as between master and pupil.

Adolf Schlatter on Method in New Testament Theology

The fellow workers of the apostles are also worthy of careful attention from the historical point of view. Mark, Luke's anonymous informant, Luke himself, and the author of the Epistle to the Hebrews should be attended to, both for the sake of finding out what we can know about what was established and generally assumed in the community, and also for their own sake. How the convictions of the community's leaders were felt in the wider circles that shared in their work is itself not without historical significance.

People who want to carve up the New Testament into a series of emergent forms will look for help from the chronology of the individual documents. This is thought to guarantee the possibility of marking off the various stages in the gradual formation of Christian ideas. If what we possessed from the teachers of Palestine was literary compositions that antedated the foundation of the Gentile church, then the chronology of the documents would really be of fundamental importance for the structure of New Testament theology. In fact, however, our documents are all contemporary with each other in the sense that they all come from the period following the establishment of the Greek church. This fact must be taken account of. The statements we possess from the Palestinians should not be evaluated without Paul being borne in mind. Beyond this it is scarcely permissible to draw conclusions about the history of doctrine from the date of the epistles. That would be to confuse statistics with history. The date of an epistle does not automatically tell us the age of its contents. It does not even tell us the period when an epistle became influential in the church. A man is older than his book, and the Johannine theology was present in the church for a long time before the gospel was written. Similarly, Paul's doctrine of justification was normative for the Greek church for a long time before Paul wrote his Epistle to the Romans. The fact that limitations are set to our observation by the meager extent of our sources, and that these cannot be overcome, must not lead us to fill in the gaps with romancing constructions. The glory of academic work is not that it knows everything, but that it sees what the witnesses make visible and is silent when they are silent.

Another question that might lead to widely differing ground-plans of New Testament theology concerns the limits of the area of research. Are there any limits at all, once one includes the task of observing the processes through which the New Testament convictions arose? Are we to think of the Palestinian or the Greek background of the Christian community? Both areas embrace not only a vast wealth of contemporary forms of both thinking and acting; in addition they are parts of a history that reaches back into a measureless past. Further, these areas that even themselves cannot be limited, are also merely parts of the total movement of human history.

As a result of the application of scientific methods to history, there has arisen a tendency to abstract all historical particularities from religious data, and to see them as a unitary thing, as "religion," which operates according to the same psychological laws everywhere, among animists as among Christians. This intellectual procedure nurtures an inclination for further leaps into the distance because the causal process that occupies the mind of the researcher becomes all the more interesting the further it stretches, and the development stands out all the more clearly, the more forms that are different in other respects can be tied up with each other through a causal line. However, we would be well advised to distinguish sharply here between what is for the time being nothing more than a construction of the imagination, and what is really the result of insight into the data. The necessary task of New Testament theology remains undone so long as it lurches up and down the wide front of the statistics and history of all religions in an attempt to establish how far back anticipations of and analogies to the ideas of the New Testament can be found. In view of the importance of New Testament theology for the church, it would be a serious loss if instead of penetrating its clearly defined area of research, it got lost in combinations that use material from all areas of the history of religions.

Scientific interests also counsel against this view of the task, because sharpness and correctness of observation are bound to suffer when they abandon the temporal and spatial unity of their object, and do not stay within the orbit of what influenced the emergence and effect of the New Testament convictions in the Christian community. For example, if the products of Babylonian or Indian religious history are brought in to explain New Testament statements, the explanation will inevitably contain a touch of imagination in it. Appeal to an alleged similarity takes the place of showing the process by which these parallels came into the Christian community. One should at least indicate some possible way in which a Christian belief of such a clearly recognizable and firmly evidenced character was able to use oriental models. It may be true that the forces that operated upon early Christianity stretch back through a long history into various areas. But the reason for their influence on the New Testament is not that they were once Babylonian, but that they had at that time become Jewish, or perhaps Greek. So the question of the synagogue and Babylon is a part of our area of research, whereas Paul and Babylon or John and India are games for fertile imaginations.

If we disregard historical processes that belong wholly to the past as far as the New Testament is concerned, and are separated from it by an impenetrable wall, there still remains the question whether we should not describe the neighboring religious areas at least in so far as they give us religious material that is contemporary with the New Testament. This might be valuable in making judgments about the causal processes. So far as I know, Lutterbeck was the first to include an account of Palestinian and Hellenistic Judaism and the religion of the areas of Greek civilization in his outline of

Adolf Schlatter on Method in New Testament Theology

New Testament theology. But these areas are themselves in need of historical investigation—especially the Palestinian synagogue contemporary with the work of Jesus and his messengers. This task is a field of its own and requires independent attention. The further we proceed beyond the present-day beginnings of the work,[3] the clearer the connections become that lead from the surroundings of Christianity to their own new formations.

If we are going to go beyond the limits of the New Testament period, then it is above all the contents of the Old Testament canon that should be considered. Otherwise the historical picture will be seriously distorted; since of all the factors reaching back into the past, none is so important as this.

If we possessed an Old Testament theology written from the standpoint of the first century and clarifying what was for the Jewish and Christian communities the content of the canon, this would give New Testament theology a valuable piece of clarification and confirmation. The possibility of such a presentation is admittedly seriously limited by the situation with regard to sources, but not even the information in the sources we have has yet been collected and worked through. However, the independence of New Testament theology remains unchallenged, even over against the prehistory that directly determines it, namely, the religious history of Israel. This is because the New Testament community is a formation complete in itself with its own central point. It grew out of a new impulse that is more than simply a repetition of old material.

We must also consider the delimitation of the field over against the later history of the church. It is true that the fact of the collection of the New Testament writings into the church's canon gives their study a practical importance that does not apply to later literature. By virtue of the fact that they are canonical, these writings have had an influence upon all generations and members of the church and have determined their communion with God. But this consideration seems to make the decision about methodology depend on our present situation rather than on the actual historical position. Is it not controlled by a dogmatic idea here? The word "canon" gives expression to a dogmatic judgment that relates the New Testament to our own religious practice. The historian, on the other hand, should be guided purely by observation of what comes from the course of history itself. The ecclesiastical literature closest to the New Testament in time seems to join on to it in a straight development. Our use of it can be further justified by the fact that the only documents preserved for us from the time between the apostles and the apologists are ones that were for some time brought into a certain connection with the New Testament. Their help seems all the more valuable in that the New Testament gives us so little

---

3. Dalman's Words of Jesus should be mentioned in first place here.

source material. The fruit of the apostles' labor is the church, as it exists in the following generations and is made present for us through its literature. It would seem that only by laying this out *in toto* can we get a complete account of the apostles' work and sufficient basis for a historical judgment about it.

But the distinction between the New Testament writings and the later literature is not based upon an arbitrary fiat. It has historical reasons. By canonizing these writings, the generations following the apostles expressed where they found that word through which the church emerged and receives for all time its connection with the Christ. They found it not in the utterances of contemporary teachers and leaders, but in the writings of these men who speak to us in the New Testament. If we obscure this fact, we come into serious conflict not with a dogma but with history. The account of a martyr's death, say that of Polycarp, was never coordinated with the account of Jesus' crucifixion, nor was a theological treatise, like for example that to Diognetus, ever valued on a par with an apostolic letter. The exhortation of a bishop never possessed the same weight as that of an apostle. We are confronted with the fact that in the consciousness of the church the work of Jesus' disciples was kept distinct from what church members with their religious gifts were able to achieve. And this judgment sprang directly from the basic article of Christian conviction, their evaluation of Jesus as the Christ. For this conception of the Christ did not spread the revelation of God equally over the whole course of history; it localized it at a particular point. That gave the disciples of Jesus an importance that the intellectual or ethical achievements of those who came later could never replace. The apostolic office only existed in the church once, and this has resulted in the distinction between their writings and everything that the churches produced thereafter.

The judgment of the church did not approve the close conjunction with the New Testament writings even of the documents we possess. Since later literature is determined by new motives that distinguish it from the aims of the apostolic word, this judgment is sound. The later literature is concerned partly with the development of church order and partly with theology. Here it is influenced by Greek ideas that are not found in the earlier period. I cannot see how presentations of New Testament theology in which quotations from the epistles of James and Ignatius, the Didache and the Pastoral Epistles, are all mixed up together, can give us genuine knowledge. This does justice neither to the New Testament documents nor to the work of the second generation. But the decisive factor in shaping New Testament theology is not where the stronger spiritual force or the loftier ethics are to be found. These differences in value recede in the first place behind concern for the facts. The reason for rejecting this mixing up of ecclesiastical and apostolic writings is that it corrects the historical facts of the matter

by reference to the historian's own dogmatic judgment. If he cannot understand why a gospel should be distinguished from other narratives, or a word
of Paul from the reflections of another theologian, this is because the notion
of the Christ is without significance for him. But that view should not be
read into the early church. That would be to misunderstand what the church
was and how it arose. Its foundation was faith in Christ. For this reason it
always stood under the word of his messengers. This is recognized by the
fact that New Testament theology has as its subject matter the New Testament, and nothing else.

Here, too, of course, knowledge of the borderland is indispensable for
the historian, both as regards what fits well with the apostolic community
and what is new and contrasts with it. The former shows how the apostolic
word continued to take effect, and the latter how it stands out against the
cultural currents of its time. But from a historical as from a dogmatic point
of view, understanding the New Testament is a task of its own.

One might again consider limiting the field in New Testament study by
reference to the concept of theology. Is the whole span of New Testament
thought part of its theology? We have theology when an idea is effectively
related to God-consciousness. So far as our picture of the world or nature
exists independently alongside consciousness of God, this knowledge can
be considered irrelevant or simply natural and fortuitous for religion and
theology. So the total inventory of our consciousness would contain far
more than belongs to our theology, and comprise statements that not only
a third person, but even we ourselves would find ineffective as regards religion. Is not the same thing true of the New Testament? We cannot avoid
the question by saying that its revelatory intention makes all its statements
theologically important, because revelation does not take place independently of men. It happens through men. The apostles' humanity is not concealed or extinguished so as to make God visible without men, over and
above them. Rather, when God is witnessed to, revelation makes the
humanity of his messengers visible and effective. Nor can the task be limited by rules set by a dogmatician: this or that is indifferent for religion—
for example, the picture of nature in the New Testament writings, or their
statements about the spirit world, and so on. These sorts of rulings may
indeed tell us what is or is not part of the dogmatician's religion. But this
is no guarantee that the men of the New Testament have been objectively
and faithfully grasped. How far the work has to be taken in this respect cannot be laid down before it is done. In the first place, the whole content of
the New Testament is to be observed. How far then the structuring shows
certain groups of statements to be only loosely connected with the theological center, or quite distinct from it, is not a preliminary question of a
methodological sort. It is in fact a result of the work itself.

Appendix C

Objections to the Explanatory Intention
of Historical Work

When the task of explanation is included in the purpose of New Testament theology, doubts about the legitimacy of the enterprise get stronger. Is not this thinking bound to deteriorate into rationalism? says the opponent. When historians explain what has happened, and that means, of course, try to give a complete explanation of it, they bring in a pile of conjectures that not only conceal the facts of the matter, but directly attack them and brush them aside for the sake of the explanation. And so the New Testament collapses under the weight of the literature on New Testament theology, just as once in the synagogue the Old Testament was buried under the Talmud and Midrash. Claiming to be alone competent to make the New Testament comprehensible, this discipline sets itself up above it, and suppresses the authority of the New Testament in favor of that of the historian.

There is admittedly plenty of evidence to show that academic work is always tempted toward rationalism, toward a pride of judgment that expects to get the whole of reality into its own intellectual grasp and so reduces it to its own field of vision. But these cheap thrills are not overcome by ignoring and despising the task of obtaining a coherent understanding. That would only produce the appearance that the unwholesome roots of the conflict lie in the very fact of a relationship between the New Testament and academic work. In fact, however, a construction that has cut loose from observation is the enemy not only of the New Testament, but also of the aims and rules of academic work. It may be that a tendency toward rationalistic conjectures that are far away from the facts clings to all academic work. But we must be continually aware that this conflicts with science as well as with the New Testament; it is irrational as well as impious. When our object is driven out by a theory that denies the real and puts our imaginings in its place, we oppose not only the past, but at the same time the ground and law of our own thinking activity, and so our own existence. In opposing the object we are also opposing the subject.

The borders between dreaming and thinking, between scientific and rationalistic explanation, are established by the laws that govern our thinking. These demand evidence in support of judgments, which means that we are here dependent upon sight and hearing that give material and basis for such judgment.

Where judgment cuts loose from the perception that is indispensable to it, where the intellect's productive power tries to be in command and play the creator so that what we produce is no longer connected with a prior receiving, where thought circles around one's own self, as though this could create from itself the material from which knowledge comes and the rules by which it is to be judged, there we have rationalism. It stands in irrecon-

196

cilable hostility to the very basis of the New Testament, because acknowledging God is the direct opposite of rationalism. But this rationalism is at the same time the road to dreamland and the death of intellectual integrity.

The danger is frequently increased by unclear theories about thought-processes that demand of academic work unlimited reliance on what thought can achieve and assert that everything that happens can be fully understood. Where this kind of postulate influences even concrete individual chains of thought, it produces apparent values in which a self finds only itself in what has happened and fixes its will in theories instead of enabling it to see. Not even the theologian, of course, will admit that there is any such thing as an absolute mystery, a thing in itself that existed unknown, without being preceded by thought and shaped by it. But he dare not confuse his own thought with God's, and so must not offend against the limits that are set, as though it were intolerable that we should also have to acknowledge what is incomprehensible. This is his protection against thinking a priori and against rationalistic construction. But every dogmatic position is tempted to this. It is found where God is acknowledged and where he is denied, in religious and irreligious colors, as orthodoxy and as heterodoxy. In all our concepts and general rules the same thing recurs, that good or bad they are only powerful when they enter real life and direct our behavior toward definite objects. This means that the dogmatician alone cannot protect the historian from rationalistic perversion of what has happened. The most important factor making a New Testament theology scientifically respectable or worthless is whether a scholar possesses the veracity of the genuine observer in concrete cases, or whether in his work he makes bold to determine the course of history to suit himself. He must protect himself against this in the course of his work by not proceeding to make a judgment before carefully and modestly perceiving, surrendering himself to the data, and never once allowing himself to judge, but first making himself feel the whole range of the conditions that produce the knowledge.

This gives the basis for answering the last and sharpest argument against New Testament theology. This objection says that undertaking to explain the word of the New Testament historically is fundamentally irreligious, whether it is then rejected or joyfully welcomed as an act which frees us from religion. As soon as we begin to discuss the origin of the New Testament convictions we have inevitably and utterly denied an essential characteristic of the New Testament, namely its property of being God's revelation. The New Testament calls God its author because Jesus speaks as Son of God and his messengers as God's messengers, no matter what the historian's own convictions may be; from this comes the interest he brings to the material. Here he investigates statements that claim to be God's revelation and derive their historical power from the fact that they have worked and continue to work as such. But concepts like being historically conditioned, development, belonging in a context, with which New Testament theology deals, seem to many people to destroy the statements the New Testament makes about itself. An act of God transcends all other causality, leaving only one dependence, namely on God. If causal connections with what went before are recognized, then a concept of the world is brought in from which the idea of God is excluded. This objection is especially lively when the evolution with its extended web of conditions reaches beyond biblical history and successfully involves its background also. The New Testament is then thought to have been made dependent upon the tarnished products of human work, Pharisaism and Hellenism, rabbinate and gnosticism, instead of on God's activity alone. It is therefore widely thought from a great variety of religious points of view that divine origin and historical mediation are mutually exclusive.

This antithesis between the idea of God and history can be proved to be false from the course of our own life and from the New Testament. Taken seriously, it tears apart the relation of our own life to God; our own consciousness is cut loose from God as radically as the New Testament is. We have in our consciousness nothing that is not conditioned by history, whether our individual history or that of the large communities in which we live and on which we depend. If history is excluded from God's influence on the grounds that it is merely transitory and human, there exists no conscious relationship to God granted us in our personal life.

As well as conflicting with our own experience of religion, this train of thought also conflicts with the fundamental statement of the New Testament. Though it often claims to be the necessary and correct sign of faith, grounded in the New Testament, in fact it attacks it at the kernel. This witnesses to God's giving, which is seriously meant and efficacious; it makes man someone who receives it, and it shapes him. God's creating and giving penetrate man's existence and consciousness in their concrete, historically determined form. It establishes him and becomes visible in and through him. God does his work of grace and judgment not outside man and so, too, not beyond history, but in it and through it. So the New Testament utterly repudiates the thesis that revelation and history cannot be united, and this at the same time destroys the view that historical research is a denial of revelation.

The argument is, of course, concentrated in our view of Jesus. As soon as Jesus is made the object of historical investigation, it appears to many people that the undertaking itself, quite apart from its particular results, involves denying Jesus the name of Christ and divine sonship. Yet precisely here, and especially clearly, God is the maker of history, not its destroyer. The sending of Jesus makes us certain that God is the maker of the man who has a relationship with him. Through him comes the history that is rooted in God's will and fulfils it. The first part of this history is achieved in the inner life of Jesus himself.

Finally, behind a negative judgment about history there stands the awareness of an unresolved opposition between man and God, and so a pre-Christian idea of God. People are afraid of God's act, as though it threatened the reality of human life. So they try to protect this reality by denying the act of God. They think that when God acts, he annihilates everything that exists besides himself. This all-absorbing God, who will tolerate no world beside himself, and who must be denied for the sake of the world's existence, is not the God of Scripture. This is how man, oppressed by the sense of God's having left him, conceives him. In fact, the relation of God to us constitutes also our relation to the world. We do not get lost from his sight by being strongly affected by what happens all around us. Nor does he get lost from our sight. In this and no other way we are his work: as members of this common life. We emerge from it in the different relationships of dependence that form us. For he gives us active life, not as isolated essences, but in the togetherness produced by historical processes.

What agencies have served to create the factors which, as the revelation of truth and grace connect us with God, cannot be established by a dogmatic certainty that the historian possessed before observing anything. The question can only be answered on the basis of insight gained in the process itself. Because we receive God's revelation through history and become what we are through it, there can be no knowledge about it independent of historical perception. How God works cannot be known apart from this. It is the essential characteristic of revelation that we see the frontiers between truth and illusion, good and evil, holy and unholy, with unmistakable clarity. If these frontiers are removed, the consciousness of God is destroyed and the revelatory value of the event is denied. But that does not remove man as a developing being, with the complexity of his consciousness and the corruptness of his will, from fellowship with God. The holy, which man is given as his own, comes by his being made holy in thought, will and nature. But how God's sanctification of him works, how far down it reaches into the profane and corrupted sphere of human history and here finds the medium for revealing God's grace and fulfilling his will, can only be learned from the facts. The incomprehensible character of a divine dispensation that sanctifies humanity arises not only in individual historical cases, but exists equally in the very fact of there being a divine ruling, calling, and sanctifying. This brings man with all the marks of his humanity into a relationship with God; it makes him capable of receiving God's revelation and bearing witness to him.

Because of the close connections between historical work and the convictions by which we live, it is inevitable that New Testament theology will be drawn into the intellectual and ethical struggle about God and Christ.

Appendix C

Every conviction has the right to try to prove itself from history and to overcome its opponents on this basis. For example, a historian may reject the idea of God, whether altogether or in the area of scientific thought, on the grounds that the latter permits only this worldy language, and sees the world as a closed system containing within itself all the conditions for its unfolding processes. But then his presentation of the New Testament annuls its central statement, and he is being quite logical when his judgment contradicts the causal links of the New Testament presentation at every step. One cannot deny from the outset the legitimacy of this account of New Testament theology any more than one can an account that proceeds on the assumption that Jesus' messianic idea is a proof of mental illness, that the messianic idea is one of many vacuous concepts in the history of religion that for a time exercise great power but then burst, and that the fact that this idea was able to take possession of Jesus' will and so achieve reality was caused by mental disturbance on his part. This sort of account makes the explanatory part of the task a resolute battle against the New Testament. It is unlikely to escape the danger of totally reshaping what happened according to the demands of the scholar's own standpoint. Every consciousness has the right to test its account by the reality we are given, and so to verify its dogmatic statement by being portrayed as the law that shapes the course of history. All the concept science demands is that no matter what intellectual furniture leads someone to make a judgment, he is clear about what factors are influencing him, and so ensures that his perception can distinguish between the part of his judgment that comes from observation of past events, and that which rests on his own immanent certainties.

Admittedly, difficulties are caused by the sharply opposing views we find in the interpretation of the New Testament and, above all, in the picture of Christ. It is widely thought that the uncertainty of historical research counts against Jesus, or at least shows the defective nature of the reports that witness to him. Since there are as many pictures of Christ as there are viewers of Jesus, and as many interpretations of the New Testament as there are exegetes, it is thought to be hopeless to seek any well-grounded judgment here. One form of this view goes as follows: one can only affirm with certainty about the New Testament history what is doubted by none of the participators in scientific research, or is at least not contested by the majority. But complaints about scientific disagreement miss the point that this is a sign not that Jesus and his word are weak, but that they are powerful. The disagreement comes from the impact of the word of the New Testament on the whole content of our ego with an energy that both gives the determination of faith to join him and evokes rejection to the point of hatred. It grasps our thinking and willing at their nodal points; the image of God with which it confronts us keeps our entire intellectual position in motion.

Adolf Schlatter on Method in New Testament Theology

Our contact with the word, therefore, provokes an extraordinary variety of points of attraction and repulse.

Thus it is not incorrect to say that New Testament theology, like dogmatics, stands on the boundary of science, and is perhaps even over the boundary, if by science one means agreement and fixed tradition and successful cooperation by many researchers leading to a unitary result. To reach agreement about the New Testament we must be united in the basic direction of our thinking and willing. That is asking a lot. It will always involve our view of nature, the will's norms, the concept of guilt, the whole content of our God-consciousness. It touches on the greatest enterprises of human discovery.

The inner peace that both scientific work and religious life need in the face of scientific argument is supported by insight into the conditions of historical work and their relationship to the job of dogmatics. We have to be clear that historical criticism is never based on historical fact alone, but always has roots in the critic's dogma, too. Also, that dogmatic or faith judgments never rest on historical work alone, because our convictions never come simply from the history that lies behind us but from the effects of that history in our experience. If we recognize the connection between the two aspects, we shall no longer use the disagreement that burdens historical research as justification for historical or dogmatic skepticism. It must be clear that as dogmatics gets from history content and justification for its statements, so too the emergence and growth of dogmatic knowledge have a verifying and purifying effect on historical judgments. Then the possibility and even relative necessity of a variety of historical efforts can be understood. They will no longer simply be accounted as the confusion of what is past or the uncertainty of its documentation. Nor will hopes be entertained of settling historical disputes by developing historical methods or gaining further results. What is needed is clarification and broadening of our dogmatic knowledge so that we can really do history which is not a useless war between an inflated self and what happened, but makes judgments that grasp the real course of events.

Precisely when historical knowledge is being directly used in a stimulating way for polemical purposes, those who share responsibility for the public state of knowledge must take care to do justice to the historical aim of New Testament theology in its simple integrity. They will not bring an end to the fight, but will see that it is fought with honorable and clean weapons.

New Testament Theology and New Testament History

If the subject matter of New Testament theology consists in the convictions found in the New Testament writings, then it differs from the historical

Appendix C

work that clarifies the events through which Christianity came into being. Even though from the side of both New Testament history and New Testament theology it is perfectly clear that they can only prosper in continuing relationship to each other, still there is intrinsic justification for a division of labor, though no separation, at this point.

Both sides must remain connected, because the New Testament contains no abstract, timeless ideas. History here becomes the basis of religion and of its doctrine. So the question of its meaning and origin cannot be answered without observing the events of which it speaks and from which it stems. An account of the history of Jesus, his messengers, and his community therefore precedes a New Testament theology and serves as its basis. At the same time, this is the indispensable tool for those whose New Testament research constructs the events it presupposes. The convictions of those working here have had a great effect upon their versions of the events. This history does not consist of deliberate changes in the situation of the community or the important individuals in it. It consists of acts that stem from their will and so are based on the convictions of those who performed them. Paul's missionary work, for example, is conditioned throughout by his faith. If an author conceals the apostle's faith by blurred ideas, he will achieve no clear picture or certain judgment about what happened through him and what made him provoke such changes in human history. Finally, no division between history and doctrine does justice to Jesus' work and death. The events of his life do not simply get a particular color from the ideas he wove with them. Their entire source and origin are to be found in his convictions. He acted on the basis of his mission in the certainty of being the Son and the Christ. So discussions of what happened through him that ignore his inner life are worthless. It would be equally worthless to list his ideas as his doctrines, independently of his experiences. Whatever of his sayings do not originate in his own experience and action come from his background in the community of his time. They are not what made him the source of a new history. To list what Jesus taught as general statements would simply add up to his Judaism, even if it included a concept of the Messiah. This shows that ahistorical constructions of the teaching of Jesus conceal the real course of history.

Both these branches need each other and move on lines that constantly make contact. But we are justified in distinguishing them because, like all other events, those in the New Testament also have a natural side that inevitably demands historical work. Even if the nodal points of this history are acts in which the actors' reason and spirit show their power, still their action belongs in the web of natural conditions that is constructed out of a host of alternating and corresponding threads. That makes the question of what happened an intricate one, and the question of the conditions that shaped it even more so. This is why the knowledge granted to the apostles is more important than the events. It is the permanent result of the history, whereas the history itself is largely forgotten and lost without trace. Their word, on the other hand, cuts loose from the turn of events and becomes a permanent power. It is this intellectual result of the course of history with which we are in the first place engaged, because this is responsible for the continuing effect of the New Testament. The dogmatician needs to know it. For the means whereby the New Testament history grasps and moves our own history is through the word that has come from it.

This judgment was already the guiding principle of the New Testament authors. They do make the connection of their doctrine with their history quite clear, but at the same time they consciously give precedence to doctrine over knowledge of events. In the texts that aim to show us the will of the Christ, his history in the sense of the chain of events can only be imperfectly obtained. Whereas the apostolic doctrine is richly documented, large parts of the career of the apostles and the early church have sunk fully into oblivion. The Johannine word, for example, is preserved in the threefold form of gospel, exhortation, and prophecy. The historical events, on the other hand, which brought about the separation of John from Jerusalem and his entry into Asian Christianity, are totally obscure, although from the historical point of view considerable importance attaches to them. The word by which Paul called Timothy to him in Rome is preserved for us; the events that preceded and followed it are lacking, although they would have contained the report of the apostle's death. The church has preserved Paul's instruction to man to be justified before God; we do have a reminiscence of his own conversion, but it gives us no complete picture of those events. This evaluation of doctrine by the first Christian generation determines also the historical work of all subsequent ones, because the latter derives its purpose and criterion from the condition of its sources. The two branches of our historical research are unequally served by these. The history of the earliest church has to be satisfied with few facts. Its main task is to clarify the holes in our view of the history that cannot be filled. We can, on the other hand, get a New Testament theology. What once was the case stands here quite clearly, even today.

Jesus can only be understood when we contemplate his history, because with him most clearly of all, thought and will, word and deed are united. Yet even here the aim of the work looks very different when it is thought to be a matter of illuminating external events, rather than of discovering the inner motivation that Jesus himself had and that he communicated to his disciples. Taking one's guidelines from the intellectual side of his history relativizes the importance of many issues that cannot be avoided in an external history.

Appendix C

Of the special subdivisions in the discipline of New Testament history, one has particular significance for New Testament theology, namely the history of the literature, or critical introduction. Judgments made about the literary history of the documents determines directly our notions about the course of the inner processes in earliest Christianity. An objection can be launched against New Testament theology from this side, to the effect that it remains a provisional and unsuccessful undertaking so long as important matters concerning the history of the literature remain in doubt, that is, for as long as there is dispute about the history of the construction of the synoptic texts; the origin of the Johannine literature in John, the disciple of Jesus; and of the Lukan writings in Luke, the companion of Paul. But it would be a quite inappropriate procedure to postpone the work of New Testament theology until the problems of critical introduction are settled. For New Testament theology is for its part an indispensable tool that critical introduction constantly uses in its own work, because a good many of its difficulties come from the inner religious history of the community. It is true that their observations that are empirical in the narrower sense, those that linguistic statistics, topography, and background, and the history of the transmission of the documents provide, are especially cogent precisely because they confront us with perceptible factuality and do not stretch down into the depths of theological work. But none of the currently disputed questions of New Testament introduction can be resolved by this sort of data. In every case considerations from New Testament theology obviously play an important role.

The relationship of New Testament theology to a discipline that has scarcely begun, namely the history of language, is similar. Earlier discussion of this was concerned only with the relationship of New Testament Greek to literary Greek; this is without significance for New Testament theology.[4] However, exact observation of the process by which language was constructed has some significance for it. This took place in the Christian community because a set of ideas that was foreign to the Greeks had to find expression in Greek. That does not mean that completely new constructions were formed or attempted. This would have contradicted the nature of language, which can only be understood when it uses materials already available, even in expressing new ideas. It would also have contradicted the aim of Jesus' messengers, which was not to invent a secret language, but to let their word be understood and done. New forms of language, however, come into existence when the Greek available has been used in the formation of new thought. This process was made easier and guided by the fact that the community thought in Aramaic as well as in Greek from the start, so that Christian construction of language in the

---

4. Even Deissmann's Light from the East is not free of the old way of seeing the problem.

Greek area followed the model of semitic constructions.[5] The transition from the language of Palestinian Judaism to Christian preaching was straight-forward. Although insight into the relation of the New Testament word to non-Christian linguistic usage, both in the Palestinian and the purely Greek area, will be of considerable help to New Testament theology, the latter is nevertheless independent of this field, because the apostolic documents are sufficiently clear to be self-explanatory. The meaning of their words is governed in the first place by their own usage. History of language for its part needs a knowledge of New Testament theology to see correctly the processes that belong to its sphere. What has changed is not in the first place, or mainly, the natural element of the language, but the thought and will of those speaking. This is what has led to a new use of language. If theology cannot get a clear picture of the overarching events, then much of what is characteristic for the development of the language remains obscure.

The close connection between the external history and the development of Christian convictions leaves room for the borders of New Testament theology to be drawn in different ways. The most complete exclusion of the historical material was effected by biblical dogmatics. When historical and dogmatic work began to be separated, New Testament theology took its questions from dogmatics, but thought that theological questions could only be answered by means of historical work, the aim of which was historical understanding. That led to the works of biblical dogmatics, which aim, to develop Christian teaching in the earliest period in a systematic way, by setting biblical statements alongside every statement in the church's system, and discussing their relationship to the ideas anchored in the church.

The interest that was satisfied by this way of working is not without some permanent justification, because the reason why historians are concerned with the statements of the New Testament is that they determine the conviction of Christianity and have produced its present theology. This methodical, deliberate, and complete comparison with what the later dogma of the church contains, provides results that are valuable for the historical picture. This is not only because in this way the influences affecting the church's dogma emerge, but also because our eyes are thus sharpened so that we can perceive the original Christian convictions more clearly. Books of biblical dogmatics are helpful to the dogmatician, too, because by this method comparison of the two trains of thought remains the firmly maintained purpose of the work, and so the evaluation of historical results by dogmatics is made easier.

---

5. Thus the question of the Semitism of the New Testament is of interest not only to its literary history but also to its theology. The question is how far Semitic forms of thought have determined the language of the New Testament.

Appendix C

The disadvantage of the procedure is that it carries over the results of dogmatic work into the New Testament and so can easily short-circuit the historical aim. The questions here are not obtained from the historical event itself, but are brought to it from the train of thought of a dogmatics that has been established at a different time. The guiding interest is directed to the church's doctrinal task, not to understanding the New Testament word. It is difficult to avoid bending this in the direction of intellectualism here. The apostles begin to look like gnostics who have an opinion about every mystery with which contemplation of the world presents us. This procedure can therefore only be applied with safety where we can presuppose that the two trains of thought are, or at least ought to be, essentially identical. When one considers that the purpose of dogmatic work is to gain knowledge, whereas the purpose of the New Testament word is beyond this to call men through God to God, and when one recognizes that dogmatic work has been and must be influenced by later situations and knowledge, it becomes advisable not to take the questions that guide the investigation from the dogmatic tradition, but to get them from the New Testament material itself.

The danger that the New Testament may be fitted to a model that is alien to it will be warded off more easily if we use as a basis for our investigation not a dogmatic system, but a simplified model of the religious phenomenon. The New Testament statements relating to those phenomena that are essential for every stage of piety and every feature of believing existence will then be gathered up. Monographs on the central Christian concepts serve this purpose. The sovereignty of God, Christ, sin, justification, love, and faith establish the content of the New Testament word. New Testament theology will always proceed in this direction because the characteristic feature of the New Testament word is that it awakens and regulates these phenomena. By applying this sort of model, the excellence of the work can be tested to see how far it is able to express the New Testament statements in their concrete, historically conditioned form.

Sharp opposition to biblical dogmatics is expressed in the judgment that New Testament theology is a misguided undertaking because the New Testament does not contain theology but religion. But this judgment only applies to people who are still unclear about the inner difference between that form of knowledge we call science and the word directed to us by the New Testament. Whereas scientific thought is not aimed beyond the intellect but seeks to construct ideas, the proclamation performed by the New Testament allows no separation of thought from the other functions that together with it constitute our existence. This is not because it occupies a lowly stage of culture and so has not yet reached the heights of scientific aims, but because it rejects and judges as monstrous a consciousness of God that remains mere consciousness and establishes nothing other than intellectual activity. It sees in God's relationship to us something that moves us totally, and so it gives us certainty of God, that we should believe him, serve him, live through him and for him. Because through God's relationship with us, knowledge of God comes to relate us to him, the New Testament is consciously and irreconcilably opposed to every form of thought that is only meant to produce a religious concept. Complete reserve toward intellectualism is an essential characteristic of Jesus' work, and it is carried on right through the apostles and in the organization of the earliest community in a perfectly classical manner. A New Testament theology that obscured this difference and described the men of the New Testament, say, on the model of the Greek thinkers or like modern academics, really would be radically perverting its material.

But there is no need to associate the concept theology with an artificial separation of thought from existence. The linguistic usage of the whole church does not require this. It does not in the least connect theology with the character of abstraction from the real purpose of life and abandoning central functions in favor of the mere construction of concepts. Thus when someone wants for the moment to set aside the more far-reaching purposes of theological work and indicate a restriction to the intellectual aspect, it is customary to speak not of theology but of academic or scientific theology. It has remained an element in the public consciousness that theology is not always or necessarily associated with a renunciation of the goals that reach down into our existence. It is worth emphasizing the strong link that theology has with the New Testament for the sake of avoiding its atrophy into an abstract scholasticism. This link does not make the concept theology vacuous or curtail it. The New Testament confronts us with intellectual activity and conceptual construction which, though not directed to intellectual goals alone, still by their energy and fruitfulness on any showing represent a high point in the movement of human thought.

The work of those by whom Christianity came into existence, from Jesus right through the apostles, was never concerned just to obtain ideas about God's government. But it is equally certain that a characteristic of their participation in God is that it was something known. It emerged through the participation of thought in God's word and will, receiving through him a rich and definite content. When we take from the New Testament the knowledge that is associated as cause and effect with Christian experience, we obtain its theology.

Theology will for a long time yet have to resist the Greek tradition as this is continued in Protestant orthodoxy, and then in rationalism and still today in speculative forms. It resulted in the fact that the whole of New Testament history was considered as merely the history of thought. This meant that New Testament theology had fulfilled its task when it had defined the concepts that the apostles attained and explained how they arose. It is a considerable scientific advance that through the reaction against speculative Kantianism, even German academic work has now become aware of the relationship between our willing and our imagination. This has resulted in a new way of inquiring about New Testament theology. But even this new current has its dangers, and needs to be protected against exaggerations. We are told that New Testament history is misunderstood when the events that determine it are taken to be achievements of thought; that the forces at work here and the great results effected belong to the sphere of the will; that it is more important to observe Jesus' feelings and apprehend his character than to ask how he conceived of the kingly sovereignty of God; that in considering Paul's assault upon the Greek world, the impulses that drove him are far more important than the formulas that he invented about the purpose of the law, the death of Christ, and the justification of believers. This shift in the direction of work is an advance, in that it frees us from the domination of an ideal of thought that was constructed outside the New Testament and was forced upon it from outside. It is true that the power of the men of the New Testament did not consist solely in their thoughts. They were able to will and act, and the way in which they were able to do this was very significant for the course of history that they brought about. The content of their thought determined the way in which they lived and showed itself to be genuine conviction by giving them their will. How it did that forms an important object for our observation.

But working like this can easily lead to the replacement of observation by free constructions of the imagination. We cannot perceive other people's will directly, but only through the ideas through which they establish their will, make it conscious, and translate it into activity. If this is not understood, imagination is given free rein to shape the historical picture out of its own conjectures that go beyond all observation, under the pretense of discovering hidden motives.

There is a science of New Testament history for as long as those engaged in it are talking about the will that moves it. This is done by clarifying through thought its grounds and goals. The object of a New Testament theology that wants to remain a science is the New Testament word. This is something given; it keeps it away from dreamland and in touch with reality. We must, however, be constantly watchful that it does not consist of abstractions, or of thought-constructions arising outside the will and real life. They must come from these and be created for them.

It is therefore not advisable for New Testament theology to imitate the modern separation between dogmatics and ethics in theology. It can, of course, be clearly recognized from the New Testament writings that the considerations that suggest this division of labor for us today were already partly operative for the founders of the church. They give their ethical admonitions a measure of independence alongside the parts that bear witness to the divine action for the world. The disciples recalled two clearly separable actions of Jesus: he instructed them about good and evil, and he showed them how God's sovereign revelation was taking place in what they saw. So, too, it is no coincidence that the ethical portions of Paul's epistles are a rounded whole at the end of the epistle; nor that alongside his gospel, powerfully written simply to establish faith, John should have written the epistles, whose entire interest is equally concentrated upon love. There was a sense for the difference that enters our thinking through its being sometimes directed upwards to perceive the divine activity, and sometimes turned inwards to the form of our own will, to construct the rules that put this on the right lines.

But both kinds of thinking, one giving a person certainty of God, the other giving him the certainties that determine his action, are consciously and resolutely united in the apostles' thought. Thus both mutually establish and strengthen each other, and are only complete when they are united. To divide up the apostles' theology into dogmatics and ethics would be a perversion of their actual material and would obscure one of its essential characteristics. The New Testament knows of no concern with the divine that does not produce ethics, because it determines our will and action. Nor does it know of a directing of our will we have to find for ourselves without reference to God. An apostolic dogmatics without any ethics would mean a falsification of it, because without an account of the action granted us by him, its statements about God and Christ would not only be incomplete; they would have lost sight of the purpose that controlled them. The behavior to which the knowledge of God calls us is not in the apostles' opinion hitched externally on to it as an addition that could be dispensed with, or as something different or new that is not essentially connected with it. Rather, this is included in God's work for the world and is indispensable for the creation and maintenance of our communion with God. Similarly, anyone who writes an ethics of the New Testament, whether it be what is called the morality of Jesus, or what may be called Pauline or Johannine ethics, comes into conflict with the reality if he gives the impression that morality is here independent of religion and exclusively a matter of the human consciousness and human will. The New Testament accounts of our obligations include the reasons for them, and this leads us not simply to individual self-contained sections of New Testament dogmatics, but to the totality of it. For example, if we produce a morality out of Jesus' words, our historical purpose goes astray if we do not bear in mind that Jesus' words on moral issues are all calls to repentance, not reflections on ethical themes. They are challenges appealing for repentance, showing its necessity and indicating its goal. Conversion to God comes about when one has the will to reach God's sovereignty and escape his judgment. Its fulfilment rests upon God confirming his sovereignty over man and acting toward him in

Appendix C

his sovereign grace. We are therefore continually confronted by the claims of Jesus upon the community's behavior, with his dogmatic convictions. Without these, his statements about morality cannot be understood. Pauline ethics cannot be described without making clear what the Christ meant for Paul, and this requires a complete account of Paulinism. Since the consideration of ethical statements always needs observation of the dogmatic reasons for them, and since, too, understanding dogmatic statements makes us pay attention to their ethical goals, New Testament dogmatics and New Testament ethics inevitably develop as a pair. It is therefore not advisable to divide the work at this point.

Appendix D

Adolf Schlatter on Atheistic Methods in Theology

Translated by David R. Bauer

All attempts to illumine clearly the point at which the theological conflict among us arises render a commendable service. So it is fitting to welcome the contribution by Paul Jäger in *Die Christliche Welt* 25 (1905). Without sentimental phraseology and with serious effort to establish a clear position, Jäger demands that theology utilize "the atheistic method." His remarks were prompted by Lütgert's statement[1] that even in historical observation and judgments God is not to be ignored; an untheological theologian would be a self-contradiction. To this Jäger replies that the atheistic method is the only scientific one: "We wish to explain the world (includ-

---

*This essay originally appeared in *Beitrage zur Forderung Christlicher Theologie* 9/5 (1905):229–50. Used by permission of the *Asbury Theological Journal*. I would like to express my gratitude to Professor Peter Stuhlmacher of Tübingen and to Mrs. Anna Kuhn for reading over this translation and offering many helpful suggestions.—Trans.

1. [Wilhelm Lütgert (1863–1938), New Testament scholar and theologian who studied under Schlatter at Greifswald in the 1890s, had delivered a paper at the Eisenach Conference in 1903 in which he challenged Ernst Troeltsch's separation of the theological and historical tasks. Jäger's essay responds to Lütgert's address. See Heinzpeter Hempelmann, "Nachwort," in Adolf Schlatter, Atheistische Methoden in der Theologie, ed. Hempelmann (Wuppertal: R. Brockhaus, 1985), 32–35.]

211

ing religion, whether its social formation or the experience of the individual) on the basis of this world," i.e., "we wish to explain it, without any recourse to the concept of God, on the basis of the forces that are immanent within the world process." In Jäger's view, then, today's dominant leitmotiv in all branches of science must function in the same way in theology. Jäger has therefore boldly countered Lütgert's remark: While Lütgert indicates that it is impossible to ignore God, Jäger answers: 'Entirely right! And we do not wish to ignore him; rather, we wish to negate him.' For whoever wishes to explain all phenomena "immanently" (on the basis of this-worldly factors alone)—whether Jesus' divine Sonship or our own knowledge of God, whether human sinfulness or the apostolic gospel—does not ignore God but negates him. Any recourse to God is here excluded not only temporarily from scientific thinking, say in the interest of producing pure, authentic observation, but is categorically banned. The essential characteristic of theology becomes blindness to God. "The scientific method," says Jäger, "*ignorat deum*, knows nothing of God."

This blindness toward God is naturally characteristic of the theologian only in terms of his scientific functioning; as a religious person he does not possess it. The religious person keeps his piety separate from his scientific endeavor. In this regard Jäger's presentation is not some new proposal that could hamper scientific observation. It is the old, sharply delineated dualism that we have long since learned from Kant, Jakobi, Schleiermacher, Fries, etc.: The heathen head and the pious heart, the atheistic scientific knowledge and the religious sentiment, etc., etc. Yet in contrast to the older attempts to split up the person, the situation has shifted significantly. Formerly the atheistic head produced things like natural science, knowledge of the world, philosophy; piety, including theology, stood alongside these as a separate domain. Now Jäger argues not merely that our interpretation of nature or epistemology is unavoidably atheistic and knows nothing of God; he says this of *theology*. The dualism which he recommends to us takes the following form: As theologians you interpret religion immanently, apart from God; as religious persons you consider it to be relationship with God. In other words, as theologians you must demonstrate what you as Christians deny. And as pious people you have to affirm what you as theologians oppose.

Logically it is entirely clear—or as Jäger might put it, "explicable in purely immanent terms"— that the older forms of dualism emerge with this harsher line of demarcation. Since religion is a part of human history and, parallel to that, of individual life-histories as well, there exists a science of religion. If science is inherently atheistic, and if it is obligated to wall itself off from the concept of God, this inevitably applies to the science of religion, too. Once one has assigned to "piety" the task of stating its views in opposition to the "scientific explanation of the world," one must also grant it the capacity to state its views in opposition to theology. But this intensifies the old dualism to such extent that it is bound to tear apart both the individual personality, inasmuch as it participates in the scientific and religious life simultaneously, and the fellowship that is peculiar to the church.

Jäger calls his article an aid "toward understanding"; this subtitle is completely appropriate, since what he writes sheds bright light on the entire difficulty of our church situation.[2] That which is still unclear in what he says merits thorough consideration.

1. Should Dogmatics Also Be Atheistic?

Jäger's answers to this question are imprecise. His final formulation of the problem ("The question we face is this: Should theology be religious science or the science of religion?") is muddled. We all support the science of religion, i.e., scientific inquiry whose object is religion. And the issue is also not "religious science" in general without determination of its object. The question turns rather on the formulation of the relationship in which science stands to religion as fact and experience. Does the science of religion affirm or deny religion? Does it dispute religion and dismiss it as illusion or give an account of it? The question centers not on isolated specifics and ramifications of religious occurrence, but on the central matter, the affirmation or denial of God. The logical confusion of Jäger's question arises from the confidence with which he puts forth his concept of science as the only possible and valid one. From the outset "the science of religion" means for him the atheistic criticism and explanation of religion. That is why he sees it in self-evident logical opposition to "religious science."

Jäger goes on to say about his science of religion: "Since science does not acknowledge God, the science of religion and therefore also scientific theology are concerned only with the subjective attitude of man. This holds true for the history of religions in general as well as for biblical and church history." Here theology is conceived exclusively as history, and dogmatics, along with ethics, is either forgotten or eliminated by a hasty amputation. Even if it be only forgotten, the fact that a theologian can speak of the superfluity of the concept of God in theology, without so much as even a thought for dogmatics, is highly illuminat-

---

2. Whoever shares Jäger's view cannot possibly be surprised if those who are deeply concerned for the gospel manifest a deep suspicion and spirited protest against "theology," and if for many in Germany it is gradually becoming a weighty question how the church can be supplied with suitable clergy, since the scientific activity of the theological faculties is becoming increasingly unsuited for this.

ing.[3] Yet the problem is not the specific formulation of Jäger's train of thought. It lies in the fundamental orientation of the approach he describes. The aims with which the dogmatician and ethicist go about their work are taboo for "scientific theology." In other words, it would be a mistake to suppose that the atheistic method of theology implies an atheistic dogmatics and ethics; these must, on the contrary, simply cease to exist. If our historical observation is thought to establish firm conviction regarding God, so that some event becomes for us a revelation of God, Jäger's response is that such "inconsistency in academic work would have to be called dogmatic method and rejected." Dogmatic and scientific are here conceived as mutually excluding opposites, and the denial demanded for the one by each component of the other is for Jäger self-evident. True, he wishes to establish for theology its rightful place within the entire complex of scientific work in the university. But his concern does not extend to theological labor in its entirety. In the university and in the sphere of science, the dogmatician and the ethicist are nothing but withered trees to be cut down.

Since Jäger wants to move us "toward understanding," it will be helpful if opponents of thinkers like Lütgert and me get a clear grasp of why we do not renounce dogmatics as a science. Emotional attachments are not what move us, as if our mood required production of some sort of conceptual literature to stay afloat. Far more important, though not yet finally decisive, is the consideration that the renunciation of dogmatics destroys religious community. There is no Christian congregation without dogma, without shared affirmations resulting in common convictions. So the question of what grounds and shapes the Christian congregation and its fellowship as a common certainty is of profound importance for every Christian. And the more unsteady and fluid the spiritual devotion of the congregation becomes, the more important the question grows. Now an opponent might reply to us: 'What kind of a narrow-minded notion this is; as if science had anything to do with praxis or theology with the church!' But such protest would reflect thinking that is really not modern at all but breathes the spirit of a past generation, one haunted and tormented by the shadow of a fanciful "pure reason" which in olden times fluttered around over reality and therefore never made connection with the praxis and the

---

3. It is also interesting that ethics is forgotten, because it documents the scant connection that exists between the theological activity called for by Jäger and the New Testament. Simply reading the Epistle to the Romans does not make anyone a Paulinist, but it is hardly thinkable that someone reading Romans could avoid colliding with the problem of the will. He would from then on be aware of questions like: What does the exercise of fleshly will involve, and what about spiritual, divine willing? How do we become free of the former and participate in the latter? etc. And whoever is gripped by such questions certainly does not forget ethics when he speaks of the goal of theology.

great social relations of life which shape us. In the contemporary university a theology would be eminently justifiable whose most earnest concern were to provide the church the theory it requires for it to be a religious community. Indeed, with their scientific work even our medical authorities and natural scientists, our economists and historians, stand in intimate relationship to "practical" tasks of the present time.

Yet in glancing at the church's need we have not yet touched the most profound reason for insisting on dogmatics. We must have dogmatics *for truth's sake.*

Jäger's reduction of "theology" to history sidesteps the truth question and thereby does damage also to the concept of science. The historian who seeks to observe what happened, and under what conditions, and what is perhaps a causal factor lying behind an event, is unquestionably obedient to the canon of truth in his work. But that same canon sets him limits. To the extent that he is the observer intent on an object, he grants the canon its power. But only to that extent: To go farther would be to suspend the canon. The canon cannot furnish him, as long as he is only a historian, unconditioned mastery. He holds his own personality in a state of suspension and abstains from forming the judgment that he might be inherently inclined to make. Thus he presents religious illusion as well as the ethically pure will, the frivolous atheism as well that faith which upholds the Protestant doctrine of justification, with the same fidelity "as a photographic camera," to use Jäger's phrase. Even the inner life of the individual is understood according to this same method: The historian elucidates how the religious conceptions arise within him; which circumstances cause them; what becomes visible, perhaps regarding causal links, between the events he scrutinizes. With this his attentiveness has borne all the fruit it can. His knowledge has reached its limits. Is his task complete? If we say yes, then we are in a cowardly way evading the truth question.

No refinement in the historian's art can alter this. We may deepen the concept of "history" ever so much; we may be realists in the highest sense in historical research and bear within us the deep conviction that what has occurred in the past affects us with causal force, that the past generates and forms us even in the course of our thinking and willing. Nevertheless, at no time are we able to grant absolute formative power over us to past events, so that the narration of that which once took place renders our own judgment superfluous, tradition replacing our own thinking and external norms of volition, acting on us from without, replacing our own volition. We remain continually summoned to an act of thought in which our own personality forms its judgment. That is a central tenet of biblical, or if the opponent does not grant this, certainly Protestant spiritual devotion. The historian, however, never reaches this point; he must maintain a suspended state of personal indecision and irresolution, so long as he is nothing but a

Appendix D

historian and knows nothing but that which took place in the past. And that is why a theology that is nothing more than history is intolerable for the Protestant church and is its death: Such theology leaves untouched its scientific obligation.

Jäger is governed by the dictum: dogmatic, therefore unscientific. But in fact the relation between the goal of historical and dogmatic theological inquiry runs in the opposite direction as soon as the truth question in its absolute form is opened up without restriction and stipulation. For a theology which can only tell little stories and thus is frozen in indecision and thoughtlessness is a farce when measured by scientific standards, even if it gives its historical novels titles like *Life of Jesus* or *New Testament Theology*. Such a theology must cower in shame when compared with the realism of natural science—but also compared with the earnestness which inheres in the history of language, of law, of the nation and the state, etc. On the other hand, if theology does not permit its goal to be attenuated and leaves adequate room for the truth- and God-question with their absolute gravity, then it stands parallel to the other branches of research in their close ties to reality. Admittedly this opens the possibility that we will also receive negative, atheistic dogmatics and ethics, e.g., a dogmatics for which the atheistically-conceived, closed-nexus concept of the world does not function solely as a "methodological" principle but is earnestly affirmed, thus transforming theology into immanent cosmology. However, a negative dogmatics, which opposes the concept of God and of course is obligated to ground its thesis in the same way as positive, God-affirming dogmatics, will always be an aid to clear distinction and decision in thinking and volition, while the reduction of theology to mere history with its endless observing and penchant for exotic non-Christian religious expression radically undermines thought and volition in the end.

2. Why Should the History of Religion Be Atheistic?

Let us now follow Jäger where his interest leads him: Why does the history of religion require the atheistic method? With welcome clarity he states his claim not as a theoretical certainty, scientific proposition, or the like, but as a decision: "We will" to explain the world immanently, so the scientific "leitmotiv" should be purely immanent in conception, i.e., conceived in such a way that the God-question may not arise at all. I call this welcome because it says good-bye to formulations like absolute science and pure reason. Jäger thus makes use of an important gain in today's understanding of the knowing process; he too is aware of the close relation between the course of thinking and willing. All thinking contains within it a volitional component, so that what "we will" appears in our science.

216

Adolf Schlatter on Atheistic Methods in Theology

In saying this, of course, none of us attributes to ourselves a sovereign power of establishing facts that is exempt from all substantiation and justification. If thinking and willing are bound together, then thinking is not denied and reduced merely to willing. For Jäger, too, "the leitmotiv" of science "is something arrived at and sustained by thinking."

The question therefore stands before us: Why do "we will" thus? In the first place, who are the "we?" Formerly, right down to the previous generation, they did not exist in the church. True, rightly or wrongly, the exclusion of the idea of God from theological observation occurred often enough; nevertheless, up until the present time there was never a theology that as a matter of principle banned the idea of God from its sphere of labor and sought to explain religion "immanently without recourse to the idea of God." Not until recently have the "we" made their debut. Jäger himself tells us as much: The type of theological work that he recommends is as a matter of principle distinct from all earlier work in the church, which he deems to have been "unscientific." Now for the theologian the unity of the church is not some trivial notion, as if the unity had absolutely nothing to do with the effort to perceive and understand with all possible diligence the transformations that have taken place in the church's thinking and willing. Commonality with the earlier work of the church takes on great weight for the theologian because of the easily sustainable observation that we, in our own religiosity, are incorporated into a common life binding successive generations to one another. In view of the whole inner situation of Protestantism, however, it is not at all surprising that Jäger facilely makes a radical break. What can the past offer to the theologian? "We cannot close our minds to the fact," says Jäger, that we have to forge a new theology, one that breaks with all that has heretofore gone by that name. So forget about the ancients, who in their unmodern unscientific way thought that they must deal earnestly with the knowledge of God in theology! "We" in the universities must internalize and further modern definitions of our goals. And why is this the case?

"We will to have a scientific theology, i.e., a science of the religious life, that stands in precise contact with the scientific awareness and labors of our time. We want to remain in touch with what is today generally regarded as scientific." The atheistic method "is the seminal scientific idea of our time."

Is Jäger observing correctly? It seems to me that here once again mists from an earlier time have blurred his vision. The absolute rationality and explicability of nature was at one time the leitmotiv for the Cartesian and Spinozan interpretation of nature. But is it really still true today that natural science is ruled by the motivating principle: "I wish to explain, and to do so on the basis of purely this-worldly factors"? Natural science wishes to *observe*, certainly also to explain, yet only so far as observation suggests causal connections to us. And that is utterly true of historical science! Where is an earnest laborer in the discipline of history who is not painfully aware of the immense difficulty involved in really seeing and observing in the face of historical processes, and how much caution is required of us to guard against cheap pseudo-explanations? The concept of the world as Jäger wields it, which he understands as a self-generating and self-sustaining unity, does not come from the observation of nature, much less from historical perception, but grows from speculative roots. It is on this basis that Jäger demands of the theologian that he undertake what every other scientific enterprise refuses, namely, to allow its operating principle to be forced upon it by allegedly omniscient speculation. In rejecting Lütgert's thesis, "In every historical method lies a hidden dogmatics," Jäger at the same time furnishes the finest evidence for it. For his idea of "world," which confers atheistic self-sufficiency on "world," so that in the entire realm of historical occurrence nothing may or can become visible except for "world," constitutes in itself a dogmatics. But it is a dogmatics that is worthless at the outset, because it is not arrived at and substantiated by explanation but rather adopted as law merely because "everyone" accepts it. "The age accepts it; therefore I must accept it, too"; that is certainly a brand-new theological method; till now such talk was never heard in the church.

We all see that atheistic tendencies are widespread in the universities. We also all see that they contain at least a measure of the earnestness of scientific verification, i.e., they are based on our contemporary view of nature and arise from careful apprehension of the discrete systems that make up the natural process as well as the power pervading that process even to the whole of the inner life. If Jäger had said: "You must explain religion on the basis of nature; everything that you call religious experience is a physical occurrence, and the concept of God is a confused synonym for nature," then his formulation would actually stand in continuity with the currents of the time. And it would likewise point to one of the great challenges that our present age poses for theological work.

But mark this. Even if we come to terms with the scientific energy that animates today's atheistic mood, and if we keep alive its power over the circle of those who labor in the realm of research and new discovery, that still gives no legitimate basis for the will that states: "We will to explain religion solely on the basis of this-worldly factors." What obligates us as members of the *universitas litterarum* [the scholarly guild] as an inviolable duty is that we, in the field of labor appointed to us, succeed at seeing, at chaste, unsullied observation, at a comprehension of the real event, be it one that took place in the past or one that is just now happening. That is the *ceterum censeo* [unquestioned prerequisite] for every labor within the university. Science is first seeing and secondly seeing and thirdly seeing and again and again seeing. From this vocation nothing absolves us, whatever else may occur in other scientific fields of labor. Let us grant that the atheistic disposition of the natural scientist arises in natural science with compelling necessity, or that the cultural historian in the course of his observations generates, legitimately and unavoidably, a skepticism worthy of Montaigne. Still, none of that would ever in itself legitimate the atheistic theologian, nor relieve us of our duty to approach our own field of labor with open observation. The fruit of colleagues' work may have the greatest significance for us, or it may create problems of weightiest, indeed impenetrable mystery. Regardless, the theologian remains obligated to regard the realm of occurrence entrusted to him with resolute devotion to his own object. He can arrive at the verdict of atheism only by way of observing the religious events themselves. If he borrows atheism from the general mood or natural science, then his position dishonors him. If theology were a know-it-all's guide to knowledge of the world like the older philosophy, then it would admittedly have to go borrowing and begging. There are, however, entirely distinct events which produce the certainty of God for both humanity and the individual. This certainty is bound up with them and works its effects through them. As theologians we owe these events an eye that is not deceived by a borrowed leitmotiv but that seeks to comprehend its object with a complete devotion to it. Even if it were true that the natural scientist nowhere found cause to arrive at the idea of God; even if it were true that the historian nowhere encountered events pointing beyond humanity, nowhere encountered a law greater than human will, nowhere encountered a judgment that breaks to pieces human will as sin; even if it were so that also in the theological domain of observation there nowhere emerged a well-founded consciousness of God, nowhere except—let us say: in the way that Jesus lived in God, here however it emerged as an undeniable reality with a power demanding assent from the theologian—in this case the basis and content of theology would admittedly be small, but atheistic theology would be destroyed. Jäger, however, does not wish to engage in painstaking observation; he knows a priori that in Jesus he is dealing only with man, just as he also knows a priori that when he encounters the sinful will in man, he has only come in conflict with a different set of human objectives.

"Theology," Jäger states, "stands on equal footing in the framework of the *universitas litterarum* only so long as it too can, frankly and honestly and not just in appearance, advocate the universally recognized scientific methods." But there are no general methods which can be transferred from one area of inquiry to another beyond those rules that are grounded directly in the way that cognition takes place. Therefore it is a general and inviolable scientific rule that every judgment must be preceded by painstaking observation, and all our own conclusions must be preceded by the act of reception, without which our own production bursts into wind and illusions. The atheistic conception of the world is not a category constituent of the act of cognition. Surely the history of recent generations proves this sufficiently. Up to and including the time of Kant's death, the concept of God was looked upon as an essential possession of reason. For the generation after Kant the self-consciousness of reason was one with the consciousness of God. Now for the "we" blindness toward God is the essential attribute of all science. Theology is too serious a matter, and it is entrusted with an area of life too significant, for it to allow itself to ape such deviations in servile deference to fleeting contemporary moods.

Jäger offers us the friendly advice "to have the resolve to withdraw from the university" since we do not find ourselves in agreement with the atheistic disposition in it. For us, too, our honor in the sphere of scientific researchers is an important regulating principle, for the simple reason that it is an effective means of work, which is what gives honor its moral worth in all relationships. But it remains for the moment an open question whether we have lost that honor by openly remaining theologians, to the extent that individual energy permits, and as theologians observing honestly and thinking valiantly. And it is far more doubtful that the atheistic theology would deserve that honor. In any case, the atheistic theological enterprise would be the most certain means of destroying the theological faculties. If it ever really comes to pass that our students read the New Testament just like they read Homer, and our exegetes explain it like they do Homer with determined elimination of every God-directed idea, then the theological faculties have reached the end of the line.

3. What Do We Lose with the Atheistic Method?

Jäger fears no loss from his method: Only the theologian would be atheistic, not his personal identity; only the method of scientific work, not the personal status of the worker; only the science, but this would be merely "the maidservant of human inquiry, not its lord" and "does not speak the last word."

But here the concept "method" contains a striking ambiguity. It merely points a "way," Jäger claims—but the choice of the way occurs here through the fixing of the goal. The proposition: "We will to explain Christ, and for that matter Christianity, both as corporate entity and personal experience, on the basis of this-worldly factors alone, without any reference to God," contains a fully determined intellectual goal which specifies the result of the entire theological enterprise. Here method does not simply furnish preliminary guidance dealing with the technique which theological work should employ. Rather it pronounces a judgment on the emergence and essence of religious phenomena. If I say: Chemistry is to be explained on the basis of physical processes, or that changes in philosophical outlooks are to be explained from the differences of climate and nutrition, these are no longer methodological principles but theories which must not be allowed to govern observation but must rather emerge from observation. Of course, I can make merely methodological use of such principles; in this case I use them to bring into sharper focus those phenomena in my area of investigation which my theories regard as the sole causative powers. There has never been a theory that cannot in turn be employed methodologically. Thus also Jäger's thesis may be employed merely methodologically. Then it says simply that we have to take account of what it signifies for the religious occurrence that it is incorporated into the cosmic, historical nexus. But we hardly need Jäger's encouragement to take this step; such methodological impulses have been fully and effectively adopted into theology for more than a century already, i.e., since the theologian too had to deal seriously with the concept of history. If that is all that Jäger intended to state, then why his polemical tone and talk of the fresh beginning of a new theological enterprise, different from all that has gone before?

But Jäger also has kind counsel for those who have accepted the abandonment of the concept of God as determinative for theology. They should still feel quite free to exercise their piety undisturbed as befits their taste and capacity. But this freedom stands on mysterious footing. The strivings of the older generation (Schleiermacher, Fries, etc.) to establish and secure such a dualism were incomparably more earnest; what we hear in Jäger gives the impression of being disorganized and lacking in profundity. So, for example, he suddenly talks again of "higher knowledge." In the old dualism this expression made tolerable sense, since it regarded only the understanding of phenomena as atheistic; alongside that understanding some "higher knowledge" might still crop up somewhere, say if alongside pure reason yet another, additional reason were discovered. But now, after even theology is to be atheistic—where does "higher knowledge" still come from? Jäger likens the results of theological labor to a photograph that captures the object at a certain angle, noting that "obviously it doesn't achieve everything." What kind of a mysterious spirit could achieve more? Would it maybe embellish the photograph or even impart motion to its image? It is true enough, as Jäger writes, that the theologian does not speak the final, most profound word. But then who does speak it? Certainly not the New Testament, for we have already "explained" it "without recourse to the concept of God."

In such an approach neither science nor religion retain what is due them. After science has first explained everything in purely human terms, it now suddenly becomes remarkably modest, more modest than is permitted if it really *explains*. First it has been demonstrated to us scientifically that our praying is obviously only a monologue. Then there suddenly comes a

Appendix D

"higher voice" that overturns the verdict of science, and science—it beats a hasty retreat. Will it really be so well-behaved and silently take its leave at the right moment? First science elucidated for us how Jesus' self-consciousness necessarily acquired its eccentric form under pressure from the ideas and tendencies present in contemporary Judaism. Yet we endorse this chain of thought only as "theologians"; we retain the freedom to believe his claim in which he designates himself the One having come into existence through God. But wait—what about science? Oh, forget about it for now. *Genuine science is not there so that we can forget about it.*

How solemnly Jäger begins: "We want a scientific theology!" Hats off to this magnificent aspiration! The appearance is given of occupying the heights of resolute love of truth, of being gripped with a burning desire for certainty and an earnest longing for reality. But where we end up does not match where we started out: Intrinsic to this "science" is a profound skepticism. It passes judgment on everything, bold, sovereign, "without recourse to the concept of God." Then it ultimately confesses that it actually does not compel any particular judgment that would amount to a seriously binding affirmation, nor does it want to.

In negotiating with Kantianism it has already been said quite clearly for a long time that dispensing with the idea of God is inevitably tantamount to dispensing with the idea of truth and is therefore destructive of science. The way in which Jäger dismisses his "science" at the moment it is convenient for him is more support for this argument.

And religion? Here too one need only repeat what has already often been said: Such a dualism makes unattainable a complete, life-determining devotion of the self to God. How can double-mindedness be avoided if the theologian and the Christian stand in irreconcilable opposition to each another in one and the same person? Greatest caution is required toward that which delivers from science, i.e., delivers from the canon of truth and earnestness for truth, working mischief in us individually and in the church in the form of feeling, opinion, "ultimate word," etc.

Of course Kant is also brought in to console us: Science has to do only with "appearance," not with "essence." But the natural scientist who breaks off his experiment, says to himself "All just phenomena!" and doesn't take seriously his results does not deserve our admiration. Nor does the historian studying Caesar Augustus or Napoleon who suddenly claps hand to forehead, cries out "Only phenomena!" and on that account grants the last word to a "higher voice" instead of to his investigation. The same goes for the theologian, who first explains religious activity atheistically and thereafter primly says: "There you are; I have explained only the appearance; think what you will about the essence." We have no other life than that which we lead as persons endowed with consciousness. In this life, so con-

stituted, a faith surrendered to God arose and continues to arise. The flight
from this life to a "thing in itself" is a sham.

4. What Do We Gain with the Atheistic Method?

It is possible to speak of an advantage only if the method is seriously employed
solely as "method." That means it gives direction to the observer's attention,
which applies itself to the relation between the phenomenon of religion and
the "world." In this respect Jäger's hopes are not entirely illusory and are in
part confirmed by scholarly methods already long in use. He can rightly say:
It would be highly instructive to see how far an interpretation would get
which contemplates religion, thus e.g. Jesus, the New Testament, the church,
our personal faith, only as a product of humans and the world. The concept
of "world" is no phantom; we also cannot measure a priori to what extent
the historical sequence of events is a closed unity. Far less can we measure a
priori how the presence and activity of divine grace and truth are mediated
within that unity. To be sure, presently the physiological aspect of the concept of "world" is still meaningless for the theologian. Questions like: Are
the religious processes contingent upon individual formations of the brain?
If so in what way? To what extent does race exercise an influence? etc., result
only in empty prattle. Such observations obtain theological significance only
when they have become an assured part of anthropology and are not just
empty words for an impenetrable mystery. It is different with those observations which are directed toward the relationship of the individual to the
people, of private thought to speech, of the individual will to the collective
will of the community, of the spiritual heritage of some present moment to
the past and the logical and ethical bonds transcending the individual which
are at work here. Along this line we have already observed much. And there
remains much more painstakingly to assimilate in the areas of biblical history, church history, and the course of individual lives, our own as well as
others. But offsetting this gain from the approach hailed by Jäger as the exclusively justified one is a vast quantity of mistakes. And the more his approach
ceases actually to be method and assumes lordship as "leitmotiv," the more
it becomes a disastrous source of error.

Observation is not an empty word; the wonderful ability to see is granted
to us, also in the historical sphere. By observation we can discern the occur-
rences that form the inner life of the human individual and of humanity.
And yet—how fragmented and divergent our contemporary theological literature, even in those matters that are determinative for our judgment on
the basis of ostensibly empirical considerations! Why? Because it is just as
certain that observation requires the use of our own eyes, and they are
informed by that which, as our intellectual holdings, exercises control over

Appendix D

us. The relinquishing of ourselves which is part of every authentic observation, which takes the form of devotion to that which has happened, can never and should never obliterate us. We are the ones who must see, and our eyes are our primary equipment for carrying out the work of thinking. That is why it is no light matter which "leitmotiv" we submit ourselves to. Now if we determine to explain religion based on solely this-worldly factors, then from the outset our observation consistently stands in radical contradiction to our object, which emphatically does not lend itself to such explanation, but loudly and steadfastly insists upon the concept of God. Our object intends that we think about God; the observer wills to think "without recourse to the concept of God." Here lies a sharp conflict of wills; if enmeshed in it, are we still able to see what lies before us? And the more we determine not merely to observe but also to explain, the more the object is shaped to fit into the scheme that we have already constructed, and the more our work becomes a caricature of science. What purports to be science transmutes into polemic against its object, and the result is not an account of the past but a novel whose main character is the historian.

Perhaps the opponent will rebuke me by calling attention to the antiquated theology which "explains" the world and Scripture "solely on the basis of God," along with that theology's historical attainments in exegesis, in christology, in the preservation and shaping of the recollections of the experiences of the church, in the biographies of the saints, etc. There, the opponent will point out, it was not the "atheistic method" that was guilty of clouding the picture of history, but its opposite. I take it to be just as little the calling of the theologian to "explain religion solely on the basis of God" as to "explain it solely on the basis of this-worldly factors." The theological rationalism of the Greeks was as mistaken with its postulates as the profane, modern manufacture of conjectures is. If we succeed at truly grasping what generates the certainty of God for us humans, how that certainty so secures itself in us that it becomes certainty and we are able to believe, how it manages to furnish us the inner motivation for will and action, so that the love of God arises and obedience springs up, and all this in such a way that not only hermits here and there in shattered isolation experience the illumination of God's light, but in such a way that the church of God comes into being—that would be theology enough for now. Admittedly such theology does not come about "without recourse to the idea of God"; it rather has its sole object and goal in him.

Briefly just a couple more matters: The invitation for us to subscribe to the atheistic method of theology has been published in *Die christliche Welt*, which takes great pains to stay abreast of the growth of Catholic theology. If one looks back at the relationship between Catholic and Protestant theology in the first half of the nineteenth century, the reversal in Catholic outlook is highly instructive. Does *Die christliche Welt* think that the atheis-

224

tic method in Protestant theology will improve that relationship? Will that relationship be enhanced by the Protestant faculties' avoidance of the truth-question, their burying the question of God and their "explaining religion solely on the basis of this-worldly factors"? If the Protestant faculties still talk of "religion," but no longer retain any knowledge of God, and their Catholic colleagues are the only ones left to pose the question of God, and they answer it by the means at their disposal (even if these are only the means furnished by Thomism), then it is likely to become obvious pretty quickly who needs help from whose theology.

And one last point: Jäger's summons has reminded us of the dignity that we possess as members of the university. As already stated, I absolutely respect this appeal to the high intellectual ideals of our universities. But it is not only to colleagues in the philosophy department that we are under obligation. As members of the university we have our dignity above all in that we stand as teachers before those studying under us. Should we turn our young people into ministers according to atheistic method? Should we face them having retreated to Jäger's position: "True, theology that has surrendered the concept of God does not achieve everything; but there are still final, deepest words beyond theology"? Certainly: There are still final words to be added to theology proceeding on atheistic premises. And sometimes they will be unwelcome words—yet sometimes words by which actually someone besides the theologian begins to speak, tearing atheistic theology, its conception of the world, and its concept of religion locked up in human subjectivity to shreds.

Index

Index

Index